Intercultural sensitivity

For
Loekie Mahdi-Hardey,
Izak Mahdi,
Maria Teresa Abondano
and Vicente Nunez

Intercultural sensitivity

From Denial to Intercultural Competence

Carlos Nunez
Raya Nunez Mahdi
Laura Popma

3rd edition

2014 koninklijke van gorcum

© 2014, Royal Van Gorcum BV, P.O. Box 43, 9400 AA Assen, The Netherlands.

All rights reserved. No part of this publication may be reproduced, stored in a retrieval system, or transmitted, in any form or by any means, electronic, mechanical, photocopying, recording, or otherwise, without the prior permission of the Publisher.

NUR 812

ISBN 978 90 232 5133 0

Cover: Kim Boeren, Viesrood grafisch & interactief ontwerp
Cover illustration: Carlos Nunez
Graphic design: Imago Mediabuilders, Amersfoort, The Netherlands
Printing: Royal Van Gorcum, Assen, The Netherlands
© Illustrations chapters 1, 2, 3, 4, 5, 7 Carlos Nunez; chapter 6 Raya Nunez Mahdi; illustrations 5.2.1 through 5.2.6 are adapted from Lewin's Circles and Trompenaars & Hampden Turner, 2008

Table of Contents

Preface 9

Chapter 1   **Cultural Awareness** 12

     1.1   What is Culture? Visible and Invisible Culture 14
     1.2   Definition of Culture 16
     1.3   Cultural Programming 16
     1.4   Culture and Subcultures 18
     1.5   Intercultural Communication 19
     1.6   Assignments 20

Chapter 2   **Working with Hall's Model of Cultural Differences** ... 22

     2.1   Communication: High and Low Context 24
         2.1.1   Low Context 24
         2.1.2   High Context 25
         2.1.3   Misunderstanding caused by too little or too much Context 27
         2.1.4   High and Low Context Countries 28
         2.1.5   High and Low Context Subcultures 29
         2.1.6   Can we Communicate High as well as Low Context? Yes 29
     2.2   Monochronic and Polychronic Time 32
         2.2.1   Monochronic Cultures 33
         2.2.2   Polychronic Cultures 33
         2.2.3   How to Succeed by Being both Monochronic and Polychronic 34
     2.3   Personal Space 34
         2.3.1   Dealing with Differences in Personal Space 35
     2.4   Fast and Slow Messages 37

	2.5	Fast and Slow Information Flow	39
		2.5.1 Slow Information Flow	39
		2.5.2 Fast Information Flow	40
	2.6	Action Chains	40
	2.7	Assignments	42
		2.7.1 Do you communicate high or low context?	42
		2.7.2 Are you Monochronic or Polychronic?	42
		2.7.3 How large is your personal space?	42
		2.7.4 Are you accustomed to fast or slow messages?	43
		2.7.5 Action Chain Awareness	43

Chapter 3 Working with Kluckhohn's Model of Basic Assumptions ... 44

	3.1	Dominating, in Harmony with or Subjugated to Nature	46
	3.2	Past, Present and Future Orientation	48
	3.3	Doing or Being Cultures: Task or Relation Orientation	49
	3.4	Individualism and Collectivism	51
	3.5	Is Space Private or Public?	53
	3.6	Human Nature	55
	3.7	Assignments	56
		3.7.1 Your cultural profile according to Kluckhohn	56
		3.7.2 Solving a Cultural Misunderstanding	57
		3.7.3 "A Day In The Life of …"	57
		3.7.4 Look at what you wrote for assignment 3.7.3	57
		3.7.5 Cultural Creativity in "A Day In The Life of …"	57

Chapter 4 Working with Hofstede's 6 Dimensions of Culture ... 58

	4.1	Power Distance	60
	4.2	Individualism	62
	4.3	Masculinity and Feminity	67
	4.4	Uncertainty Avoidance	69
	4.5	Long-Term Orientation	71
	4.6	Indulgence and Restraint	73
	4.7	Country scores on Hofstede's Six Dimensions of Culture	74
	4.8	Assignments	76
		4.8.1 Your Cultural Profile According to Hofstede	76
		4.8.2 Assignment: The Curriculum Vitae	76

Chapter 5 Cultural Synergy: Trompenaars' 7 Dimensions and Cultural Reconciliation ... 78

5.1 Universalism – Particularism. Rules or Relationships? ... 80
5.2 Individualism and Communitarianism ... 82
5.3 Emotions: Neutral and Affective ... 82
5.4 Involvement: Specific and Diffuse ... 84
5.5 Status: Achieved and Ascribed ... 91
5.6 Time ... 95
5.7 Attitudes towards the Environment ... 95
5.8 Reconciliation: from Vicious Circle to Virtuous Circle ... 96
5.9 Three steps to Cultural Synergy ... 102
5.10 Assignments ... 106
    5.10.1 What is your cultural profile according to Trompenaars' 7 Cultural Dimensions? ... 106
    5.10.2 Work in pairs. Read case 5.1 of the driver and the pedestrian ... 106
    5.10.3 Specific and Diffuse ... 106
    5.10.4 Cultural Synergy Assignment for Health Care ... 107
    5.10.5 From your own experience ... 107

Chapter 6 The Growth Process in Intercultural Sensitivity ... 110

6.1 Denial ... 113
    6.1.1 Strategies for moving on from the denial stage ... 113
6.2 Defence ... 115
    6.2.1 Strategies for moving on from the defence stage ... 115
6.3 Minimization ... 117
    6.3.1 Strategies for moving on from the minimization stage ... 117
6.4 Acceptance ... 119
    6.4.1 Strategies for moving on from the acceptance stage ... 119
6.5 Adaptation ... 121
    6.5.1 Strategies for developing even further when you are in adaptation ... 121
6.6 Integration / Intercultural Competence ... 123
6.7 Assignment ... 124

Chapter 7 Culture Shock While Studying Abroad ... 126

- 7.1 Culture Shock. What is it? ... 128
- 7.2 What are the Stages of Culture Shock? ... 128
- 7.3 Pre-Departure Stage ... 131
- 7.4 The Vacation Stage ... 132
- 7.5 The Angry Stage ... 133
- 7.6 Adjustment Stage and Strategies ... 134
- 7.7 Re-entry Shock ... 135
- 7.8 Assignments ... 137
  - 7.8.1 What You Leave Behind ... 137
  - 7.8.2 Your Comfort Zone ... 137
  - 7.8.3 Creating New Strategies ... 137
  - 7.8.4 Your Fellow Students in Culture Shock ... 137

About the Authors ... 138

Bibliography ... 140

Preface

This book is a first approach of what can happen at the university or business schools where students of all nationalities and cultures come together.

You are going to read an enlightening testimony on what could happen to you students when working later in companies, without being aware of the content of this book.

The authors most warmly thank **M Luis Miguel Rojo Y Pinto** for sharing his field experience with the students.

"With both parents from Spanish origin, I was born in France and considered myself as being a pure multicultural product, till I had to settle in Latin America a few years ago. That's where I got my first real "intercultural slap" while having a meeting with Columbian engineers. As we were looking into security issues for our vehicles, my purpose had been to concentrate on the necessity to fit them out with series airbags and ABS. One of them just replied that security was essentially linked to the engine power, which was vital to overtake on the overcrowded roads of this magnificent country.

This anecdote cruelly brought me back to the notion of context.

Another example: when a Marketing team in Venezuela presented me with a very interesting project, I let out a vibrating "Not bad!" which made the Project Manager immediately turn pale and asked me why I didn't like that project. This was all a question of interpretation, "Not bad" in Venezuela is a polite way to say you refuse the project. Consequently, when working for a Korean brand, I had to change the way I defended and presented the projects to the Korean executives, presuming that it was impossible for them to lose face opposite their counterparts with the same power distance, even if I had previously succeeded in obtaining their agreement. All a question of culture.

I am now working with Nissan, in a Regional Business Unit, bringing together France, the Netherlands and Belgium. It is a daily concern to me as I am confronted to the difficulty to adapt communication patterns in order to align multicultural teams and meet shared goals. Strange as it may seem, a French "yes" is not necessarily interpreted in the same way as a Dutch "yes". There is no such thing as a universal way of applying the filters we get from our upbringing, our social environment or our experience. Even if we are used to global environments and we have the feeling that we do know "the world" through all kinds of media and tools at our disposal, we are not always aware of the need for decoding the messages. In that case, we have to use our counterparts' references and not ours.

This book is based on real examples and exercises and enables the reader to, not only understand why the exchange of messages that seem clear are not understood, but also to ponder on questions about his own story. In each chapter you will find basic principles which throw a light on the differences in interpretation between cultures. Take some time and hindsight to consider those aspects and you will most probably avoid blunders that can sometimes cause violent shocks. Those are more often related to the use of an inadequate form rather than to a disagreement on the content."

Luis Miguel Rojo Y Pinto, Marketing General Manager, Nissan West Europe

1 Cultural Awareness

Introduction and Definitions

1.1 **What is Culture?**
1.2 **Definition of Culture**
1.3 **Cultural Programming**
1.4 **Culture and Subcultures**
1.5 **Intercultural Communication**
1.6 **Assignments**

In this chapter we will define culture and intercultural communication. Culture is learned. Culture influences the way we think, feel and behave. It even shapes our perception and influences our judgment of others. We are not always aware of the impact of culture on the way we communicate. The aim of this chapter is to become more aware of our own culture, how it influences our communication, and how we can become better intercultural communicators.

1.1 What is Culture? Visible and Invisible Culture

According to the interculturalist Edgar Schein culture consists of layers, like an onion.

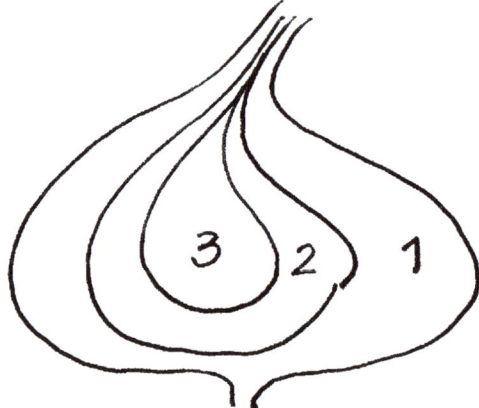

Illustration 1.1 Cultural onion.

1. Artefacts of Culture
2. Norms and Values
3. Basic Assumptions

1. The outer layer, or material culture, we call *artefacts of culture*. Artefacts are the first things you notice when entering a new country. Foreigners arriving in the Netherlands notice: the bicycle lanes, large windows and open curtains, the tall people, and how they dress. They notice that a lot of Dutch people eat bread and drink milk at lunchtime. The first time you enter a new company, you'll notice the artefacts: company logo, company house-style, and whether or not the employees wear ties. Artefacts are easy to perceive, and they're nice to know, but intercultural communication is not going to be about artefacts.

2. The second layer we call the *norms and values*. They are written and unwritten standards of correct, desired behaviour. Is it the norm to arrive in class a few minutes early, exactly on time or is it the custom to be a few minutes late? Is 3 minutes late acceptable and 10 minutes not? These are examples of norms. Values express what we think is good or right. For example, is it good to stand up for an elderly person on a crowded bus? Is it right to send a card or make a phone call to a classmate who is ill? Norms and values are not as visible as artefacts. It takes some time to notice, let alone learn them. But with the necessary effort and observation, they can be learned.

3. The deepest layer are the *basic assumptions*. They are abstract and invisible, we learn them very young - before we are 7 - and we are unaware of their influence. Yet the perception of the world around us, and the judgements we make about others, are very much shaped or distorted by the basic assumptions of our culture. Intercultural communication is about bringing basic assumptions of our own culture to our awareness and to recognise the basic assumptions of other cultures. This is in order to communicate creatively and more effectively with people from other cultures, to use cultural diversity at work as a source of inspiration and growth, and to achieve *cultural synergy*. In chapter 5 of this book we will present a 3-step strategy on how to achieve cultural synergy.

Illustration 1.2 Cultural iceberg and the Titanic as metaphor of cultural clashes on the invisible level of culture: the basic assumptions.

1.2 Definition of Culture

This book is not going to be about Culture with the capital C such as literature, art, music, theatre, museums and architecture. It is about culture with the little c. It is about the familiar way we think, feel and behave. How we learned this and share the meaning of it with other members of our society. The list of definitions of culture is endless. The table below gives 4 definitions. We have chosen this short definition by interculturalist Geert Hofstede:

> *Culture is the collective programming of the mind, which distinguishes the members of one group ... of people from another.*

Definitions of Culture

Edgar Schein defines culture as... "A pattern of shared basic assumptions that the group learned as it solved its problems of external adaptation and internal Integration, that has worked well enough to be considered valid and therefore, to be taught to new members as the correct way to perceive, think, and feel in relation to those problems." (Schein: 2004)

Mijnd Huijser defines culture as ... "A group's set of shared norms and values expressed in the behaviour of the group's members." (Huijser, 2006)

Fons Trompenaars: "Culture is the way in which a group of people solve problems." (Trompenaars, Hampden Turner 1998)

Geert Hofstede: "Culture is the collective programming of the mind, which distinguishes the members of one group or category of people from another." (Hofstede 1991)

1.3 Cultural Programming

Culture is learned. Hofstede calls it *programming*. You could also call it "learning", like Edgar Schein does. We are programmed through upbringing, socialisation, norms and values, and perception.

A lot of programming comes with our *upbringing*. Take a simple handshake. There's nothing natural about it. No child would dream of shaking hands unless it was programmed to do so. "Be a good boy, be a good girl now, shake hands."

This is repeated and drilled so often that you end up thinking that shaking hands is normal.

A lot of other things we learn through *socialisation*, by interacting with others. To stay with the handshake, do you give a limp handshake? A firm one? A crunch? Through socialisation you learn just how firm a desirable handshake is, and even the right smile and amount of eye contact to go with it. In Europe, a firm handshake is desirable. And you would associate a limp hand with weakness of character. In many Asian countries, firm handshakes are seen as aggressive, and people find a modest, gentle handshake more polite. We are also programmed through *norms and values*. If we value showing respect for older people, and the norm is to give your seat to an elderly person on the bus, you will feel good when you stand up for someone older, and feel uneasy if you don't. In some countries the norm is to give up your seat to children, because children are small and vulnerable.

Finally, part of the programming happens through *perception*. Just by looking around us we make conscious or unconscious choices about how we want to behave.

Does programming reduce us to cultural robots then? No. Regardless of culture, each person is a unique individual and makes choices, for example, to follow or to deviate from the cultural group norms.

There are three levels of programming:

Individual
Cultural
Human Nature

If we haven't eaten for days, human nature makes us look for something to eat and devour it with our hands! That we decide to put the food on a plate and eat it with fork and knife is our cultural programming. However, individuals may chose not to use fork and knife, regardless of their cultural programming or what society thinks. Similarly, in some cultures, your programming teaches you always to share food with others and never to eat on your own. There too, individuals may chose to eat it up all by themselves, regardless of the community's disapproval or possible sanctions.

Now let's move on to the word *collective*.

1.4 Culture and Subcultures

In "Culture is the collective mental programming of the human mind", *collective* indicates the group or subgroups we belong to. It does not mean that the whole country is one big group, or shares one set of cultural patterns. On the contrary, there are a lot of subgroups or subcultures we belong to: a regional culture, middle class culture, or company culture, each with their different programming.

Here is a list of possible subcultures

- A continent (Asian culture, American culture)
- A country (The Dutch culture, the Polish culture)
- Ethnic (The culture of Ethnic minorities in Holland, such as the Indonesian, Surinam, Moroccan or Turkish culture)
- Regional (The culture of Brabant, Friesland)
- Urban or rural (Culture of the Randstad)
- Religion (Catholic, Protestant, Islamic, Jewish, Hindu or Buddhist culture)
- Social class (Middle class culture for example)
- Gender (Differences between the culture of men, women, also the gay culture)
- Age (Culture of young people, of the baby-boomers, or the pre-war generation)
- Profession (Health-care-, engineering-, or economics and management culture)
- Hobby (The culture of hockey, soccer, stamp collectors, chess-players, or gardeners)
- Corporate (Differences between cultures of the Hogeschool Rotterdam, Hogeschool Utrecht or Utrecht University)

The list is fairly complete, but not exhaustive.

It is good to be aware of differences as well as similarities and overlaps in our subcultures. Dutch and international students at the Hogeschool Utrecht, involved in a management-simulation-game called Intopia, found that their professional interest was such a uniting factor, that it helped them transcend their initial national and regional cultural differences. They worked together out-standingly.

Culturally diverse teams. The worst or the best? Both. If left unmanaged, culturally diverse teams can have a lot of problems understanding each other and coming to an agreement. If managed and trained in intercultural communication, they turn out to be the most creative and dynamic teams.

1.5 Intercultural Communication

Communication is the exchange of meaning. If you want to give information to another person, you are the source. Your information is encoded by using the appropriate language, gestures or nonverbal expressions. It is transmitted through a channel, which is the medium for communication. In face-to-face verbal communication it is the air and the space between you, if it is written communication it is paper, with emails the medium is electronic. The receiver decodes your message and responds, once again encoding the response. You decode it. All communication takes place within context, for example, in business context or family context. A crisis situation is another context. Noise can distort the message, whether it is external noise (sledge hammer, neighbours' TV) or internal noise (worried about the telephone bill or nervous about your first speech).

You can also have cultural noise, meaning that cultural programming can distort the message. The right voice volume for speaking professionally in Holland might be too loud for Indonesians, thus distorting the message. The appropriate amount of eye contact in one culture may be too much for another culture. This distortion of the message is caused by cultural noise.

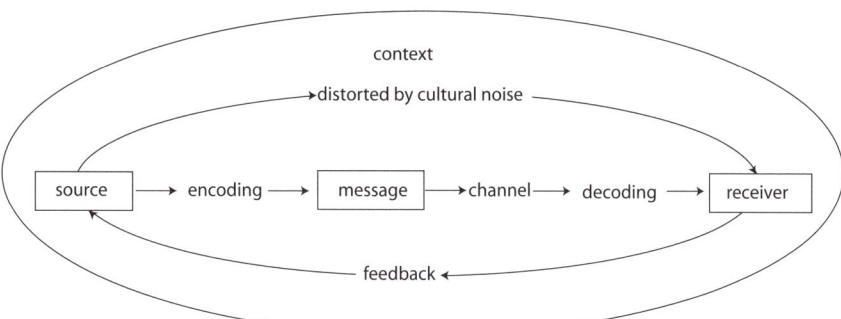

Illustration 1.3 Intercultural communication is the communication between sources and receivers from different cultures.

In this chapter we have defined culture and cultural programming as well as cultures and subcultures. We have identified layers of culture and distinguished artefacts of culture from norms and values and basic assumptions.

In the next chapters, we will define basic assumptions. But first, we would like you to take the first step in intercultural communication by identifying your cultural programming and your cultural groups. You can do this with the following assignments, preferably with a student from another culture, subculture, gender or age, or you can try to do them on your own. Discover the differences as well as similarities between students from other cultures.

1.6 Assignments

1. Culture

Take a blank sheet of paper. Write "Culture" right in the middle of the paper and circle it. Think of "Culture". What jumps into your mind? Write down everything that enters your mind. Don't worry if it's wrong or right, don't judge. Keep writing till you've filled the page. Till nothing else pops up in your mind. Till nothing else flows out of your pen. (Adapted from the module Intercultural Communication, KIT, Royal Tropical Institute, Amsterdam)

2. Layers of culture

Take three different coloured highlight markers, say green, yellow and orange. Take the result of assignment 1. Highlight everything on that page that is tangible, or an artefact of culture, in orange. Use the yellow highlighter to mark all things related to norms and values. Is there anything on your paper that might fall under basic assumptions? We will discuss basic assumptions in the next three chapters.

3. Layers of culture

a. Give a few examples of artefacts of culture.
b. Give some examples of norms and values.
c. Can you already give an example of a basic assumption?

4. Collectives and Subcultures

Work in groups of 2. In Hofstede's definition "Culture is the collective programming of the human mind", the word "collective" stands for group. To which "collectives" or groups do you belong? Tell each other who you are and which groups you belong to. Talk about your family. That's a group. About your friends, where you come from, where you lived before, where you live now. Your neighbourhood, the cities or countries you might have lived in. Tell about your previous schools. What sports clubs or hobby clubs you belong to. Do you belong to a religious organisation? Notice that these are all subcultures that you are bringing to your awareness. Talk about the familiar behaviour of the people in these groups. How do they greet each other in your family, in your group of friends, at your old school, in your neighbourhood, town, and country? How do the people in these groups behave towards people from outside the group?

5. Programming

How were you programmed? What did you learn and from whom?

Make a colourful chart, or map, of all the subcultures you belong to and compare it with your group mate. What is different? What is the same?

a. Work in groups of 2. Tell each other a few things that you learned at home and at school. And who taught you.
b. Now give three examples of what was considered good behaviour. (For example, setting the table, or clearing the table after dinner, coming home on time.)
c. How were you rewarded for that good behaviour? (With a smile, or "thanks"?)
d. What was considered bad behaviour? (For example, not saying "thank you" when they offered you a cookie. Or not telling the truth.)
e. How was bad behaviour discouraged? Was there punishment?
f. Name the most important thing that you received through your programming, something that you will one day pass on to your own children.

2 Working with Hall's Model of Cultural Differences

2.1 **Communication: High and Low Context**
2.2 **Monochronic and Polychronic Time**
2.3 **Personal Space**
2.4 **Fast and Slow Messages**
2.5 **Fast and Slow Information Flow**
2.6 **Action Chains**
2.7 **Assignments**

In this chapter we will show you how to use the theories by the American anthropologists Edward and Mildred Hall to make your day-to-day intercultural communication more effective. The Halls compare culture to a gigantic, finely tuned computer. The computer programmes work wonderfully, just as long as you do all the actions in the right sequence. This is something you do automatically without thinking. What happens if you skip even one single action? It won't work. Communicating in a different cultural setting is like working with a computer programme that needs different action sequences. People will say about the computer: "It doesn't work", or of the culture: "There is something wrong with them".

Of course there's nothing wrong with the computer or with the culture. We just need new tools to work with other programmes (and other cultures). To start with, we need to get acquainted with our own cultural programming and value the cultural programming of other cultures.

Edward and Mildred Hall use a set of 6 tools, called key concepts, for more effective intercultural communication:

1. High and Low Context Communication, 2. Monochronic and Polychronic Time, 3. Personal Space, 4. Fast and Slow Messages, 5. Fast and Slow Information Flow, and 6. Action Chains.

By the end of this chapter you will be able to make your personal and cultural profile according to Hall's Key Concepts.

2.1 Communication: High and Low Context

Illustration 2.1 Context: High or Low?

All communication takes place within a certain context. But how much or how little meaning is communicated through the context itself differs from culture to culture. We distinguish high context and low context communication. Note that high or low does not mean better or worse. Both communication styles are just as good, but very different.

2.1.1 Low Context

In low context cultures information is communicated explicitly, with words. Words, written or spoken, are important in communicating the message. Furthermore, in low context communication, people prefer to structure their information into segments, or "compartments". This is called compartmentalising. Personal relations, work, and everything else you deal with are also compartmentalised. Information has a clear structure, but it doesn't flow very fast, because it remains within the compartments. Consequently, when people meet each other they need detailed and specific information.

A low context culture has a preference for starting with the main point and ending with details.

In the Netherlands, where we launched this book, the norm is to communicate low context and explicitly. That doesn't mean that everyone in the Netherlands communicates in low context, but most people do.

2.1.2 High Context

In high context cultures most of the message is in the persons themselves and in the context of the message (what surrounds the message). So not everything is spelled out explicitly with words, but implicitly and often nonverbally. One word, gesture or hint at the context is enough to understand the whole picture and message! Context includes "the total picture" such as history, social background, relationship, status, atmosphere, time of day, the place, and the person who is communicating. People in high context cultures live in large communities. They have access to wide networks. Personal networks and business networks flow over into naturally intermingling spheres. These liquid networks keep you informed of what's going on. So when people meet each other, there is less need for specific background information.

A high context culture has a preference for starting with context, (which sounds like details to low context listeners) and get to the main point later. In fact, main points are not compartmentally separated from details, but they form one holistic picture.

What happens if high context messages are transmitted to people accustomed to getting their information compartmentalised and low context? Before reading on, please do case 2.1.a "Introduction: A house".

Case 2.1.a Introduction: A house

Take two minutes and work in pairs with a classmate or colleague. Both of you think of a house – any house, yours or someone else's. Take turns describing it to each other and take one minute each.

Feedback:

Could you get a clear impression of the house your classmate described? Did your classmate get a clear impression of yours? What was clear? What information was missing for your classmate to get a clear picture of your house?

Table 2.1 Results with Dutch students.

> When we asked 54 Dutch students to describe a house as in 2.1.a, these were the most frequent descriptions:
>
> - Four walls, a pointed roof, front door, back door and four windows.
> - A house. Two storeys, four rooms, with a south-facing garden.
> - A large semi-detached house with a garage, drive way and huge garden.
>
> The descriptions were sometimes followed by very explicit details of the interior:
>
> - an open kitchen, with a dining area
> - bathroom with a bathtub and a shower
>
> Some continued to described the atmosphere in great detail as well:
>
> - When you walk in, there's a table and a mirror.
> - On your left, the living room with a cosy fireplace.
>
> These are classical low context descriptions, all starting with the main point (a house). Details came later. And if the context was mentioned, it came at the end (drive way, garden).
>
> When asked whether the descriptions were clear, most students said yes.

Table 2.2 Results with international students.

> When we asked a group of international students to describe a house as in exercise 2.1.a., these were some of the answers from students from high context cultures, respectively Kenya, Spain, Morocco, China and Japan.
>
> - It is located in a big garden in a compound. The roof is iron. The walls are of bricks. The floors are of cement. From the entrance you go into the living room, and on the first floor there are some other rooms. The kitchen is outside.
> - It's an apartment. In Barcelona, in a very nice area, not so far from the centre. It's not too busy and very modern.
> - It is in a beautiful lane, with rows of large and very old trees. The old couple who used to live there were famous artists. Their paintings are in the museum. After they died, their daughter sold the house.
> - There are many nice people in the house. Father, mother, grandparents. People eat together. When I come home, the light is still on.
> - In Japan we have a lot of earthquakes.

2.1.3 Misunderstanding caused by too little or too much Context

Looking back at the last five house descriptions, you can imagine that people who are used to receiving explicit, compartmentalised and low context information can get irritated by them. Instead of the house and its walls, the roof, and number of rooms, they talk about Barcelona, grandparents and earthquakes!

On the other hand, people from high context cultures need to receive messages within a context - human context, physical context, or historical context. They too get irritated when people from low context cultures go straight to the point with explicit details. When the whole context is missing, it's hard to follow. You can't "place" it. Four walls, and a pointed roof is not a clear description. Where is this house? In a quiet tree-lined lane? At a busy junction? Who lives in it? Is it safe (from earthquakes)? They might also get irritated when people from low context cultures give them information that they already know from their extensive networks.

Too much information sounds belittling. Too little information is unclear, or makes the recipient feel left out. Intercultural sensitivity means to be able to provide the right amount of context and explicitness. It's not about being either high or low context. It's the ability to understand and communicate high and low context. It is the ability to hear, "Japan has a lot of earthquakes", and understand, "This house has strong foundations, walls, and roof; made to withstand frequent earthquakes". See 2.1.6 for more strategies.

This table sums up the characteristics of low and high context communication.

Table 2.3 Characteristics of Low and High Context Communication.

In low context communication, the message ...

- is verbalised explicitly
- is clearly structured, in separate "compartments"
- is direct
- is more literal (less metaphorical)
- places more emphasis on the spoken as well as written words
- places less emphasis on non-verbal communication
- starts with the main point, and then moves on to details

In high context communication, the message ...

- is part of the person, thus, it is not always verbalised explicitly
- flows freely instead of staying within compartments
- is indirect, aimed at not being blunt, not hurting feelings and creating consensus
- is coded so that you interpret it metaphorically
- transferred non-verbally is as important as the verbal message
- starts with the context, circling towards the main point, sometimes zigzags between details and main points

2.1.4 High and Low Context Countries

High and low context are not black-and-white opposites, but relative. Furthermore, you can be high context with friends and low context at work. There may be overlap.

Having said that, and making room for differences in subcultures, you could place low context cultures in the Anglo-Saxon, Germanic linguistic areas. This means North-Western Europe, North America (USA and English-speaking Canada), as well as Australia and New Zealand.

Countries in Central and Eastern Europe are in a way, "medium context". Compared to North-western Europe, they are high context.

We find the high context cultures in Latin Europe (the French, Spanish, Portuguese, Italian speaking countries), countries around the Mediterranean, the Middle East, Asia, Africa, Latin America and Oceania.

2.1.5 High and Low Context Subcultures

Within one country, there is a whole range of differences in the need for context, depending on the regional, urban, rural, ethnic, social class, professional, gender and generational subcultures. In the US, low context is the norm, but Latinos in the US are high context. In the multicultural Dutch society, people from Antillean, Indonesian, Moroccan, Surinam or Turkish background are high context at home and low context at school or work. In the end, they are good at both high and low context communication. People in rural areas can be higher context than in urban areas. Women communicate higher context than men. The older generation prefer higher context than the young. Professional culture and corporate culture have differences in need for context.

Remember, these are generalisations. They are descriptive and not evaluative terms. And we need to recognise individual differences from the country-norms. Your individual experience and personal programming can make you very different in your need for context compared to other people in your culture, gender or age group.

2.1.6 Can we Communicate High as well as Low Context? Yes

What if you are basically low context, talking to someone high context, who just doesn't seem to understand what you're explaining? Are you going to repeat it, but simpler? That won't help. Simplifying will just deprive him of even more context! Try a different strategy. Start with a bit of context. Mention a place, historical background, or your personal involvement. Now watch for the "Aha!" look in his eyes. Then you may give the explicit main points. Case 2.1.b is a real life example of how this works.

What if you are basically high context, and your low context listener has difficulty following you? The more personal, historical context you add, to "clarify", the more confused he is getting. Change strategy, quick! That main point that you were saving for the end, start with that main point right away. Say explicitly what you mean. Don't depend on your subtle nonverbal hints. Say it literally with words. Spell it out. If you absolutely need to say something about the context, keep it brief. Leave details for the end. See the real life example in case 2.1.c.

Intercultural sensitivity

Illustration 2.2.

Case 2.1.b A Dutch student on Internship in Jakarta
Anne, a Dutch Marketing student from Utrecht University of Applied Sciences, is on internship at an Indonesian company in Jakarta, Indonesia. On one of her first days at work, Anne tells her Indonesian colleagues all about her Marketing Studies in Utrecht. She tells them it's a 4-year study, what subjects and projects she has, and what her career prospects are. Nobody seems to understand what Anne is talking about. And it's not because of the language.

So Anne explains all over again. She adds explicit details, such as the number of credit points she gets for each subject, and what the total number of credit points she needs to complete her main phase studies. No use. The Indonesians are even more "lost".

"They're not interested", Anne thinks, "I give up." And she escapes to the canteen. Yanti, an Indonesian intern, joins Anne for coffee. Yanti wants to know all about Anne's studies, and asks, "How old is Utrecht University? Is the building old? How many students does it have? Are the lecturers friendly? How big is Utrecht? Is it an old city? What kinds of sports are popular among students in Utrecht? Do you like sports? Do you like salsa?" Context, context, context.

After lunch Yanti tells all her colleagues. Now everyone at work knows how nice Anne is, and how interesting Anne's Marketing studies are! Anne now plays basketball in Yanti's club, and feels completely at home.

Question 2.1.b

a. Describe your studies, using low context, explicit communication.
b. Now describe it again in such a way that it would interest Yanti! So, high context.

Case 2.1.c A Russian Exchange Student in the United States

When American professors ask a question in class, they expect students to give short, to the point, explicit answers. In other words, low context. If you give high context answers, the professors think you don't know and are rambling around in circles, trying to guess.

An American professor asks a Russian student, Sergey, "What are the characteristics of low context communication?" "Thank you", Sergey opens, "for this very interesting question. Low and high context", he adds, "is terminology developed by the American anthropologists Edward and Mildred Hall...." "Go on", the professor prompts. "They wrote about it", Sergey continues, "in their book: Understanding Cultural Differences. They describe six key concepts ..."

By now, the lecturer has lost interest in the answer and has moved on. Another student completes the answer. Sergey gets an insufficient participation grade.

Question 2.1.c

You are Sergey's coach. Sergey does not understand why he got an insufficient mark for his eloquent answer, which was bluntly cut short.

1. Give Sergey a few golden tips on how to formulate his answers low context, in order to communicate better with his American professor and fellow students.
2. Imagine that Sergey gets a second chance to answer the question in the case. He follows your advice. Write down how Sergey's answer should be......

2.2 Monochronic and Polychronic Time

Taking our personal or cultural assumptions about time for granted is one of the greatest obstacles in intercultural contacts. There are many different time systems. An important basic assumption of time is what Edward en Mildred Hall call monochronic and/or polychronic time. (From mono, one; poly, many; chronos, time; meaning one thing at a time or many things at a time. Not to be confused with single or multi-coloured monochrome or polychrome with which most computer spelling-checks tend to replace monochronic and polychronic)

Table 2.4 Characteristics of Monochronic and Polychronic Cultures.

In Monochronic Cultures:

- You prefer doing one thing at a time
- You concentrate on your tasks and try not to disturb others
- Time is linear; you take deadlines and time schedules seriously
- Your communication is low context
- You need explicit information
- You are task oriented
- You do your work swiftly and promptly
- You make plans and keep to them

In Polychronic Cultures:

- You prefer doing many things at the same time
- Interruptions aren't really interruptions; you can still carry on with what you're doing now or later
- Time is spatial; deadlines and time schedules can be kept to, if possible
- Your communication is high context
- You don't usually need explicit information, because that's what your network is for, to keep you informed up to the minute
- You are relationship oriented
- How swiftly and promptly you work depends completely on how good the relationship is
- You make plans and change them with the greatest ease and flexibility

Adapted from Understanding Cultural Difference by E. Hall and M. Reed Hall, 1990.

2.2.1 Monochronic Cultures

In monochronic cultures, time is experienced linearly, as a long road leading from the past through the present to the future. Monochronic time can easily be segmented into blocks of time, which is what we do when we plan our time in our business diaries. Hall and Hall call this "compartmentalisation". That makes it possible to concentrate on one thing at a time, and to plan time. For monochronics, time is sacred. Things that happen according to plan are good. Time is tangible. Monochronics talk about time as if it were money. It costs time. You can gain it, save it, and waste it. You can even lose it. And since monochronics like to concentrate on one thing at a time, they don't like to be interrupted. It's not polite and not efficient for the gears and clockwork of monochronic progress. Monochronics are champions in keeping deadlines.

In which countries is it the norm to keep to monochronic time? Similar to the low context countries: the Anglo-Saxon, Germanic linguistic areas: North-western Europe, North America (USA and English-speaking Canada), as well as Australia and New Zealand.

In monochronic cultures, relationships are also compartmentalised.

2.2.2 Polychronic Cultures

People in polychronic cultures live in a sea of time. Time moves spatially, in all directions, rather than linearly. Polychronics prefer doing a lot of things at the same time, and are more concerned with people than with planning.

It is more important to let a conversation take its natural course than to interrupt it, because you will otherwise be late for an appointment. Time is elastic. Time adjusts itself to your needs. For polychronics time is not a tangible commodity, and it is not the clock, says Hall, that dominates the life of polychronics.

Polychronics are perfectly capable of combining a lot of activities at once, follow several conversations simultaneously, and do not find interruptions a problem.

Where are the polychronic countries? Similar to the high context countries: Latin Europe, Latin America, the Mediterranean, the Middle East, Africa, Asia, and Oceania.

Central and Eastern Europe combine monochronic with polychronic time. So do the industrialised Northern Asian countries.

2.2.3 How to Succeed by Being both Monochronic and Polychronic

Monochronic or polychronic: again one is not better or worse than the other. They are both perfectly functioning systems. But let's face it, they're not compatible. But they can be complementary. Being aware of how your cultural programming made you prefer monochronic or polychronic time, and by not assuming that your preferred time is universal, you have made a big step in intercultural sensitivity. If you are accustomed to monochronic time, polychronics may appear to be impolite, chaotic, and even untrustworthy. This is far from true. Before judging, let's discover the boundless opportunities of polychronic time. Discover the polychronic in yourself. Take a break at work, and drop by your polychronic colleagues or fellow students for a chat. Genuinely try to get to know them better, let them know you better. It's fun. And it increases your personal network and mutual trust. And that is the very basis of polychronic efficiency. For a friend, polychronics will do everything: even keep deadlines.

If you are accustomed to polychronic time, monochronics may seem inflexible, inefficient, and cold. This is also far from true. Discover the efficiency of monochronic time. And how this efficiency will result in your having even more time to spend with your friends. Keep a business diary, use it and keep it up to date. Write down all your appointments in it. Not just the person you are meeting. Also the time and place you are supposed to meet each other. And be there, exactly at those times. Your monochronic fellow students, colleagues and lecturers will feel appreciated if you keep to your appointments. And it increases your mutual trust. Monochronics feel better and more relaxed when work is finished on time, according to schedule.

2.3 Personal Space

Besides having skin as a visible physical barrier between our bodies and the outside world, human beings also have an invisible barrier that we consider our personal space.

We feel uneasy when other people get too close and trespass into our personal space. They are not keeping the correct distance. How large this personal space is differs, depending on the situation and relationship – strangers keep a larger distance than colleagues and acquaintances, these in turn keep a slightly greater distance than friends and family – but it also depends on culture. In low context countries in the north, personal space and correct distance can be quite large. This can differ from half an arm-length in the Netherlands, more than half an arm-length in Germany and Scandinavia, to almost a whole arm length in the USA. Take a look around you, at people waiting at the bus stop, at the supermarket. How far do they stand from each other? Is it half an arm length? More? Do they touch? Probably not.

In high context countries, more to the south, personal space is smaller. People stand closer in Spain, even closer in Morocco, and almost touching in Indonesia.

2.3.1 Dealing with Differences in Personal Space

How do we react when other people stand too close or too far from us? Most of us aren't aware that we even have a personal space, let alone how large it is. It's one of the basic assumptions we learned at such a young age that we take it for granted. So our reaction to people taking the wrong distance is unconscious and automatic. If they are too close we feel threatened or insulted, and assume the intruder is aggressive. We automatically take a step back, which clears the air, because we have just corrected the personal distance. If they stand too far from us, we also feel uneasy, rejected and left out. They seem cold.

With people from our own familiar culture, profession, social class, etc., we know exactly what the right distance is and don't have to think about it. When crossing cultures the distance is new, it's an adventure.

To be interculturally sensitive when it comes to space, it is important to be aware that personal space is part of our cultural programming. It is not universal and we should be aware of what our own correct space preference is. So if a person from another culture seems aggressive or cold, it could just mean that their familiar personal space is smaller or larger than ours.

Cases 2.3.a, 2.3.b and 2.3.c are examples.

Case 2.3.a "They stand so far away"

In his Just Act Normal. 99 Tips for Getting Along with the Dutch, Hans Kaldenbach advises ethnic minorities on how to interpret the correct personal distance. Hans Kaldenbach explicitly said that his book is written in the masculine communication style. It is aimed at ethnic minority men:

"Dutch people talking to you, stand further away from you than you are used to. They think it is intrusive to stand at the normal Turkish, Moroccan or Surinam distance. If you notice that a Dutch person you are talking to takes a step back, then he doesn't feel comfortable. You are too close. If a Dutch woman thinks you are standing too close to her, she might think you have sexual intentions.

Dutch people don't touch each other while talking. If you do, you'll notice that they don't like it. They think you are homosexual. Or they assume you don't know how to behave."

From Doe maar gewoon. 99 Tips voor het omgaan met Nederlanders by Hans Kaldenbach, 2004, page 7.

Case 2.3.b "Excuse me"

In his bestseller, Dealing with the Dutch, Jacob Vossestein advises expatriate managers how to interpret Dutch behaviour. He also wrote a Dutch version of it, Zo werkt dat in Nederland (That's how it works in the Netherlands) aimed at making Dutch managers aware of how expatriate managers interpret them.

Jacob Vossestein's tips for Dutch managers include:

- Try to be more gallant, even to men
- Say "excuse me" (to Americans) if you accidentally almost make physical contact.

From Zo Werkt Dat in Nederland by Jacob Vossestein, 1998, page 117.

Questions for discussion

1. Why do Americans say "excuse me" if they haven't even touched you? (only almost touched you)
2. As they have to be explicitly advised to say "excuse me", we assume it isn't the custom in the Netherlands to say this. Why is it not the custom for Dutch people to say "excuse me" if they only accidentally almost touch you?

Case 2.3.c Intimidation in class

This is a real case from a Dutch University in Rotterdam. Names have been changed. Rob, a Dutch lecturer in statistics gave students back their corrected and graded assignments during his class. One of his Dutch students of Moroccan background approached Rob with a question about his grade. Rob felt very intimidated, and filed a complaint. When the student in question was called to explain his behaviour to the confidential counsellor, he was too astonished for words. Intimidation? He had no idea his behaviour had caused Rob distress. "I only asked if he could explain my grade."

Questions for discussion

1. Using the intercultural communication tools or key concepts from this chapter, explain what was going on. Why did Rob feel intimidated? Why didn't the student realise he was intimidating?
2. Imagine that you are the interculturally sensitive confidential counsellor. You have invited the lecturer and the student to listen to each other's story. They are sitting in front of you, and have each politely listened to the other's story. How are you going to solve this?
3. How are you going to avoid this happening again?

2.4 Fast and Slow Messages

Remember the communication model in chapter 1 about coding and decoding messages? Fast messages are those that we can decode very quickly. Slow messages take a longer time for the source to decode. The very essence of a slow message is that it is decoded and experienced slowly. Almost everything can be placed somewhere along the spectrum of the slow-to-high-message-speed. Fast messages are, for example, headlines, TV commercials, e-mails, memos and text messages. They are supposed to be decoded fast. Easy informality is also a fast message. Slow messages are things like poetry, art, philosophy, TV documentaries, books and letters. A painting by Van Gogh of a hundred years ago, is still being decoded, and interpreted today. If someone writes you a poem or a letter, you are supposed to absorb it slowly. Formality is also a slow message.

Most of us are not even aware that we can send messages at different speeds. And we are not aware that messages that can be fast in one culture need to be slow in another (Including the subculture of age and gender). If you send a fast message to someone who expects a slow message, or the other way around, your message will not be received correctly.

A stranger is slow message, because it takes time to know a person well. How slow or fast you get to know someone differs from culture to culture. What we actually mean is, how slowly or quickly do you release personal information?

Jaap and Patrick, two Dutch students on vacation in America remarked, "Americans are incredibly friendly". In America, people are geared to faster messages and the easy familiarity is not difficult for Americans. While on the move during their vacation, Jaap and Patrick appreciated this form of fast message. Although the Dutch young generation is also geared to relatively fast messages, compared to Americans, the Dutch messages are slow. When Patrick returned to America to do a three-month internship, he complained, "The Americans are so superficial." He expected deeper friendships with his American colleagues, who, friendly as they were, regarded him as a nice acquaintance. There is nothing superficial about that. It is just a difference in speed of messages.

When CNN started to broadcast in Europe, many Europeans said CNN news was superficial. The news was broadcasted at the normal American speed. Nowadays, they broadcast at a slower speed. Everything but the sports programmes. For a taste of real fast messages try watching sport on CNN!

Message speed and easy familiarity also poses a problem when sending and receiving e-mails (see case 2.4). The art is to watch for nonverbal as well as verbal feedback, to check whether the message you sent is reaching its target. And to adjust your speed, use of language and formality to the receiver's speed.

Case 2.4 Kristian Darmanto

Kristian Darmanto, from Indonesia, is a student at the International Business and Management Studies at a Business School in the Netherlands. He wants to make an appointment with one of his lecturers, Otto van Jasperen, to talk to him about promoting the school in Indonesia. He sends the following e-mail.

Dear Sir Otto

It is an honour for me to address you with the following question. I would greatly appreciate it if you would kindly make your valued time available to me for a matter that is of great importance for the future of the school in general, and for the internationally renowned department, IBMS, in particular. As you know, our school is highly regarded in Indonesia for its standard of education. And many parents would gladly advise their sons and daughters for a future career in International Management. Thanking you in advance for your generosity in making your time available,

With kind regards,

Kristian Darmanto
(1st year student)

Questions for discussion about context and speed of messages

1. How would Mr. Van Jasperen interpret this email?
2. Why would the message completely miss the receiver?
3. The message is deeply hidden in the context. But there are clear clues in the direction of the implicitly hinted at message (real, unwritten message: May I make an appointment to talk to you about promoting our Business School in Indonesia) Could you name the context information that clearly points in the direction of the message?
4. You are Kristian Darmanto's classmate, and friend. Explain to him why Mr. Van Jasperen is not going to understand this e-mail.
5. Help Kristian rewrite the e-mail so that Mr. Van Jasperen will be enthusiastic and invite Kristian for an appointment right away.

2.5 Fast and Slow Information Flow

Besides the speed in which messages are decoded, messages can also reach its target faster because it is unrestricted, or slower because it is trapped in cultural barriers known as compartmentalisation.

2.5.1 Slow Information Flow

In low context countries such as the Netherlands, information is compartmentalised; information stays within departments and doesn't flow freely. We call this slow information flow. People actually prefer information to remain within departments. When they want information to be shared by other departments they organise interdepartmental study days and other networking events. So to be informed, people are briefed. In the USA, another low context country, information flow is also slow because directors sit in private offices guarded by a secretary who protects the director's territory from information overload and prevents more information from being shared, whether inward or outward.

2.5.2 Fast Information Flow

In high context countries such as China, France, Spain, Morocco, Turkey, Indonesia, Somalia, Surinam and the Antilles, information moves about as if "it has a life of its own". And people live in a "sea of information" (Hall & Hall, page 23). There is a minimum of schedules and screening by secretaries and private offices, and a maximum of trying to keep up to date on information. People move in huge networks and share information naturally with friends within those networks. All it takes is one visit to the coffee machine, water cooler or restroom for an employee from one department to be up to date on what is happening in another department. The lunch break is enough for news to travel between friends working at different companies. The rest is transmitted over dinner, or at cafés.

In a way, information flows freely in Holland too and people in Holland also have networks. But it is the norm to keep information compartmentalised, controlled and planned. More cross-departmental information sharing would be seen as unprofessional gossip.

Case 2.5 Friends Forever!

Three Chinese students had been friends since their first year of studies in electronic engineering. They lived together in one student's house, had meals together and studied together. If one was ill the other two shared their lecture notes with him. If one had problems the other two helped. But when it was exam time they competed for the highest marks. After graduation, one was appointed to work at Philips in China, the second at Sony – China and the third at Samsung – China.

Question for discussion.

What could you expect to happen here, from the point of view of information flow?

2.6 Action Chains

An action chain is the sequence of events in which people work together to achieve a goal. If one step of the sequence is omitted, rushed, delayed, or performed by the wrong person, you will not achieve the goal. Everything we do has its established action chains. Enrolling for a study, opening a bank account, reserving audio-visual equipment at school, returning a malfunctioning cell phone, making an appointment with your supervisor, or asking friends over for dinner.

The steps in the action chain can be technical, such as enrolling for your studies. But they can also be so generally accepted, such as how to make an appointment or invite someone for dinner, that we are unaware of the action chain. Until we unconsciously apply the same action chain in a multicultural setting, which requires more (or fewer) steps, and different players. If we don't achieve our goal, we are tempted to blame the other culture. It is more effective to question the sequence of our action chains, and renew them.

Case 2.6 Exam Action Chains. The Exam Board and Exam Post-Registration

Context: At most universities all over the world, students have to register for the classes they wish to attend. Once registered, they are entitled to do the exams as well. At many universities in the Netherlands, however, there is an interesting tradition. Students need to register for the classes, and several weeks later, they also need to register for the exams related to these classes. There is a reason. Administration needs to know how many exams to print. If you don't register, you may not do the exam. Under special circumstances, the school's Exam Board may grant a student permission to do an exam anyway. The Exam Board then "post-registers" a student – which means exam registration after the closing date.

Case: At an international department of a University of Professional Education in the Netherlands, members of the Exam Board were complaining about the huge number of foreign students who forgot to register for their exams. After the closing date for exam registration, the Exam Board was swamped with letters from foreign students requesting the Exam Board to post-register them for the exams. The Exam Board spent hours rejecting the requests, pointing out that it was the students' responsibility to register on time, by themselves. The students were horrified. They called it a useless tradition. They were enraged by the lack of understanding for the loss of time this was causing them. Not to speak of the costs of delaying their exams till the next term.

It doesn't take a genius to solve this problem. Especially when knowing about action chains.

1. Describe the action chain for doing an exam at a University of Professional Education in the Netherlands (every step needed).
2. Ask a student from outside the Netherlands to describe all the necessary steps, or action chains needed for someone to do an exam in his or her country.
3. Use the difference in action chains to explain why the Exam Board has this problem, all year, every year.
4. Suggest a solution (Don't forget to include knowing how many exams to print).

We have discussed six key concepts by Edward and Mildred Hall, and illustrated them with examples from students' and lecturers' real life experiences. Your next step is to do assignment 2.7: Making your cultural profile according to the basic assumptions or key concepts by E. and M. Hall.

2.7 Assignments

Cultural Profile according to Halls' Key Concepts.

2.7.1 Do you communicate high or low context?

Look at your description of a house, at the beginning of this chapter. Would you classify yourself as high, medium or low context? Place an I in the space for yourself. Place a C in the space for most people in your culture. You may differ from your cultural norm.

Low Context		Medium context		High Context	

2.7.2 Are you Monochronic or Polychronic?

Place an I for yourself and a C for most of the people from your culture below:

Monochronic		Medium mono- and polychronic		Polychronic	

2.7.3 How large is your personal space?

Stand next to a fellow student and talk about the meals at the school canteen. How much space is there between you? Repeat this with 2 or 3 other students or colleagues. Mark I for yourself. Watch how close people from your culture stand. Mark a C for them.

1 arm length	¾ arm length	½ arm length	a bit less than ½ arm length	¼ arm length	less than ¼ arm length	touching

2.7.4 Are you accustomed to fast or slow messages?

Place an I for yourself and a C for most of the people from your culture below:

Fast			Medium			Slow	
Always fast	Almost always fast	Usually fast	Medium fast	Medium slow	Usually slow	Almost always slow	Always slow

2.7.5 Action Chain Awareness

a. Choose one goal from the list below, and describe the action chain in detail.
b. Ask someone from a different country, or who has lived in another country, to describe the action chain sequence for that goal in that other country.
c. Imagine you were living in that country. Cross out in red the sequences that are too many. And write in red the sequences that are missing in your action chain.
d. Write a conclusion to this action chain awareness.

Goals:

1. Enrolling for a study
2. Opening a bank account, (current or savings account, whatever you choose)
3. Reserving audio-visual equipment at your school
4. Returning a malfunctioning cell phone
5. Making an appointment with your supervisor
6. Asking a friend over for dinner

3 Working with Kluckhohn's Model of Basic Assumptions

3.1 **Dominating, in Harmony with or Subjugated to Nature**
3.2 **Past, Present and Future Orientation**
3.3 **Doing or Being Cultures: Task or Relation Orientation**
3.4 **Individualism and Collectivism**
3.5 **Is Space Private or Public?**
3.6 **Human Nature**
3.7 **Assignments**

This chapter will present the studies done by cultural anthropologist Florence Kluckhohn. We will give you practical examples of how to illustrate the way cultures differ on six basic assumptions. And we will give you tools to bridge the differences.

Edward and Mildred Hall, of chapter 2, placed emphasis on cultural differences in communication. Kluckhohn's starting point is that all people, all over the world, and throughout the ages, have had to deal with a number of problems in order to survive. People all over the world have to eat, dress and find shelter. They have to communicate with each other. How do they stay healthy? How do they educate their young? How do they organise their government? They have a limited number of choices to deal with these problems. In every culture there are several alternatives, but people prefer certain alternatives over others.

3.1 Dominating, in Harmony with or Subjugated to Nature

How do you manage your day-to-day problems? Dominating, in harmony or subjugated to nature?

In nature-dominating societies, people survive by changing the environment to meet their needs. They solve their problems systematically.

In societies that are in harmony with nature, people survive without drastically changing their environment. Some problems they change and solve, some they don't. And so they survive by accepting some of their problems and adapting to them.

In societies that are subjugated to nature, people completely accept their situation, and this is their preferred survival strategy.

Illustration 3.1 A nature-dominating solution to living on land that is below sea level. Windmills to pump the water out; dykes to keep the water out once and for all.

CHAPTER **3**   Working with Kluckhohn's Model of Basic Assumptions

Here is another common problem: a leaking tap. In nature-dominating cultures, leaking taps will quickly irritate, so you call the plumber or try and fix the tap yourself. Leaking taps are not likely a source of irritation if you are from an in harmony-with-nature culture. You might just place a bowl under the tap, and forget about it. Or you might decide to fix it some day.

Besides a natural environment, we also have to deal with our business, social, political and other environments. A conflict with a colleague at work? Talking it over with your colleague, and solving the conflict would be the obvious thing to do in nature-dominating cultures. In in-harmony-with-nature societies, you would tend to ignore the conflict. It'll blow over.

Dominating, in harmony with or subjugated to nature, one isn't better than the other. They are all effective ways of surviving. But they are very important assumptions to be aware of, especially in the Netherlands, where we wrote this book.

Illustration 3.2 An in harmony-with-nature solution to living on land below sea level. Houses in Thailand/ Malaysia /Indonesia built on poles right in the water. The problem is not removed; people adjust their lives to the problem.

The Netherlands is nature-dominating (see illustration 3.1), and we mean it positively. A lot of foreigners in the Netherlands complain that the Dutch are always so busy solving problems that they're constantly looking for problems that aren't even there. But that's because the Dutch are so good in problem solving, that they anticipate problems, solve them before they arise and by doing so avoid them. The major horror for Dutch people working abroad is to see houses with their paint peeling off the walls, light bulbs missing from lamp fixtures, rusted cars, and other problems that they could so easily fix. "Why doesn't someone do something!"

3.2 Past, Present and Future Orientation

A society can be mainly past-oriented, present-oriented or future-oriented. It can also be a combination of all three. This can have a great impact on what you consider to be reasonable time-planning, while others find it much too soon or too far in the future.

In past-oriented cultures, people evaluate plans according to how well they fit with their traditions. People are inspired by historical events. Relating to the past is an indication of the importance of a matter. In present-oriented cultures, plans are made for the short-term. Traditions and events from the past may also be important, but you don't dwell on them for too long. Living for the moment is central in present oriented cultures. Future oriented cultures are goal oriented. That goal may lie in the near, far or distant future. Time-orientation can vary between cultures (see country-time-orientations in illustration 3.3). One of the reasons why Western companies fail when forming joint ventures in Russia, is their disinterest in the Russian history and Russian past. A missed opportunity.

But there are also differences within the same culture, between people of different professions, regions and age groups. Economists in the Netherlands are more future-oriented than people in other professions. They use future-orientation in making cost-benefit analyses to predict what impact government policies will have in the next 5 or 10 years.

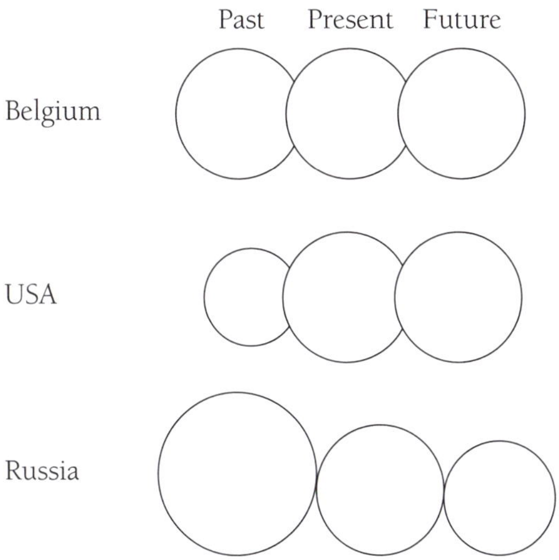

Illustration 3.3 Time-orientation.
Illustration from Riding the Waves of Culture by F. Trompenaars and C. Hamden Turner, 1998, page 127.

3.3 Doing or Being Cultures: Task or Relation Orientation

Are you efficient because you are task-oriented or people-oriented?

In doing cultures, people are task oriented and "live to work". The USA is a doing culture. So is Germany. The Netherlands is too, but slightly less extreme. Australia and China are also examples of doing cultures.

In being cultures, people are more relationship oriented, and "work to live". Indonesia, the Caribbean, Surinam, Turkey, Morocco, Spain and Mexico are a few examples of being cultures.

This basic assumption has an enormous impact on how people experience their work. In doing cultures, people set goals and take action. They set parameters to measure and evaluate the outcomes of their action. They feel highly motivated by a job well done. Managers motivate their staff by offering promotion, personal growth opportunities, a raise in salary, more responsibilities, extra vacations or other forms of recognition. It is no surprise that a doing culture as the US produced Motivation Theorists such as Maslov and Hertzberg (see Herzberg's Theory in table 3.1).

In being cultures, people, events and ideas flow spontaneously (Adler, page 29). Being people are highly motivated by the enjoyment of being with friendly colleagues. A raise in salary is welcome, but does not necessarily lead to increased effort. Employees may even decide to work less, because after getting a raise, you can earn the same as before in fewer hours. Managers can encourage their being-oriented staff to make greater effort by being caring and considerate. If employees don't enjoy their work or colleagues, they quit.

Table 3.1 Theory of Herzberg.

Illustration 3.4.

According to Herzberg's Motivation-Hygiene Theory (1991) employees are motivated by internal factors such as the work itself, responsibilities, promotion and personal growth.

External factors such as friendly colleagues, salary, and nice supervision are okay to keep you going, but fail to energise, satisfy or motivate you.

Now that may be true in doing cultures, such as the USA, but only in a few segments in being cultures, if at all.

3.4 Individualism and Collectivism

The Netherlands, Germany and the USA are individual-oriented. Individual independence is a highly priced value. In individual cultures you define yourself with personal achievements – your own name, what you study, or what your job is – and you are concerned with your own welfare and of your direct family members, rather than with the larger group.

Collective societies value inter-dependence, a sense of belonging and responsibility towards the group. In a collective society you define yourself as member of a community, referring to your father, mother or grandparents' names as well as yours. You refer to their professions as well as yours. Your welfare is one with the group's welfare. By saying "family" you mean the extended family. Your reference group includes classmates and neighbours.

In individual-oriented cultures, parents teach their children at a very young age to be I-oriented and independent. Tie up your shoelaces yourself, help clear up the table, and earn your own money. You are respected for your individuality. At school and university, teachers encourage students to study by themselves, solve problems themselves, and write papers in their own words, express their opinions. Depending on others for help is a sign of immaturity.

In collective societies children learn to be we-oriented. Interdependence on each other is so highly valued that the word "individual" is a synonym for egoist. Someone who does things on his own is pitiful, or a misfit. People enjoy asking each other for help (see table 3.2).

Needless to say, individualism and collectivism are both just as good. They each have their strengths as well as weaknesses. Successful organisations use individual and collective values in defining their vision and mission. They reward employees for collective behaviour (team work, coaching new employees, supporting colleagues) as well as for individual behaviour (taking initiative, creating new concepts).

Table 3.2.

Illustration 3.5.

After studying in the Netherlands for 6 years, Manuel from Bolivia returns to Cochabamba. As family members from all over town gather at Manuel's welcome-home-dinner, Manuel proudly tells all about his experiences: learning Dutch, working nights to pay his tuition, studying on his own, fixing leaking taps by himself and even cooking his own meals!

His aunt's comment wiped the smile right off his face.

"What?" She gasped, "Cooked your own meals? Studied on your own? Didn't you have any friends? What is wrong with you? Why didn't any one want to study with you?"

"Why work evenings?" his uncle asked in disappointment. "Why didn't you tell us you needed money? You have family. We could have helped you!"

"Son," his mother asked after the guests had left, "Did you have to embarrass your father and myself on your first evening home? As if we couldn't help pay for your studies!"

3.5 Is Space Private or Public?

Cultures differ in their use of physical space. At one end of the spectrum, there are cultures where a lot of space is private. Your own room, own desk, own car. At the other end there are cultures where a lot of space is public, and very little is private. In between the two extremes you'll find cultures with some private and some public space.

As a student, can you just walk in your lecturers' offices? Do you have to wait outside till they say "Come in"? Is entrance restricted to walk-in hours?

In Northern Europe and North America, people value private space, and private offices. Even if you share an office, you like to have physical or visual partitions between the desks. There is nothing good or bad about this. It's a preference. Private space also communicates a message of respect. People who are seen as important have very much private space, or even a private office.

In Asia, space is more public. In many Asian countries, offices are open and shared by many employees, open-plan offices. Directors may have separate offices. But in Japan, superiors often sit in the same large office as the employees. But they do of course have the place of honour, such as the seat facing the door and farthest from the door, or with other symbols of rank.

What people consider private domain and public domain can differ greatly per country, but also according to other sub cultural differences such as gender. Men may see opening someone's handbag as, well, just opening a handbag. But to many women this is a tremendous breach of privacy.

Table 3.3 Private space exercise.

> Try doing the following private territory test with someone from another culture or gender!
>
> - Mark an X for the areas and objects in the first column that are out-of bounds (without your special permission) for the people in the first row below
> - Compare your answers
> - Discuss the differences

Intercultural sensitivity

These places and objects marked X are out of bounds for...

		My Girlfriend Boyfriend or Partner	My mother	My best friend	My colleague or fellow student	An acquaintance	A stranger
Kitchen							
Toilet							
Handbag							
Car							
Desk drawer							
Fridge							
Bedroom							

Adapted from Culturele Waarden en Communicatie in Internationaal Perspectief by Claes & Gerritsen, 2002, page 79.

3.6 Human Nature

Are humans basically good, basically evil or a mix of both?

Societies that believe that people are basically evil have a tendency to distrust people. People live in houses with locked doors. This value is reflected in theory X management, where managers believe that subordinates basically dislike work, so they must be controlled, supervised and punished in order to perform (McGregor, 2006).

Societies that see people as basically good are high-trust-societies. People don't lock the doors of their houses. Managers prefer theory Y management, assuming that employees are basically responsible for their work and are innovative (McGregor, 2006). So the most effective way to work is by sharing responsibilities and decision-making with the employees, rather than controlling them.

Societies that see people as a mix of good and evil believe in the possibility for people to improve through training.

Although this value doesn't necessarily apply to one specific country, it can help explain differences in behaviour within societies. Kluckhohn herself did not identify countries. Canadian Interculturalist Nancy Adler mentioned the Puritans as an example of those who see people as basically evil. She sees Americans as viewing people as a mix of good and evil. She calls the Inuit in Canada (still referred to by many as Eskimos) examples of people who see humans as being basically good (Adler, page 23-24).

> ### Example: The Inuit in Canada Set Doors Ablaze
> Perhaps because people fear the unknown, they frequently tend to assume that evil intentions motivate foreigners' behaviour. Canadian government officials, for example thought that Inuit, a native people, were evil when they burned down the doors in Canadian-built public housing projects. The officials misinterpreted the Inuits' behaviour as vandalism, and therefore judged it to be evil. Whereas the Inuit had actually altered the houses to fit their normal – doorless – lifestyle.
>
> The Canadian government condemns the destruction of property.
>
> The Inuit condemn closed doors that separate people from family members and neighbours.
>
> *From International Dimensions of Organizational Behavior by Adler, 2002.*

In this chapter, we have discussed the basic assumptions according to Kluckhohn. These value orientations are by no means static. They can vary within a country, depending on context (private or business), gender or profession.

Now it is time for the third step on your path to intercultural sensitivity: Discover your personal basic assumptions based on Kluckhohn's value orientations, by doing the assignments in 3.7.

3.7 Assignments

3.7.1 Your cultural profile according to Kluckhohn

Are you more doing or being? How do you solve your day-to-day problems? By dominating nature or acting in harmony with it? These are not absolutes, but can vary in intensity. Mark an I for yourself, and a C for the norm in your country

Dominant or In Harmony with Nature

Dominant			In Harmony			Subjugated

Doing or Being

Doing						Being

Individual or Collective

Individual						Collective

Past, Present and Future Orientation

Past			Present			Future

Private and Public Space

Mostly private						Mostly public

Are humans basically good or evil

Basically good						Basically evil

3.7.2 Solving a Cultural Misunderstanding

Think of a situation you have been in, where a misunderstanding happened between you and someone of a different culture. Could you now explain what went wrong, using Kluckhohn's basic values?

3.7.3 "A Day In The Life of ..."

Describe a typical day in the life of a student at your school

3.7.4 Look at what you wrote for assignment 3.7.3

a. Underline all the activities that are doing, individual and dominating over nature.
b. In what way would the day be more effective, enjoyable or less stressful, if the activities were more being, collective and in harmony with nature?

3.7.5 Cultural Creativity in "A Day In The Life of ..."

Now re-write "A Day in the Life of" above, with both doing and being, individual and collective, dominating and in harmony with nature aspects.

4 Working with Hofstede's 6 Dimensions of Culture

4.1 **Power Distance**
4.2 **Individualism**
4.3 **Masculinity and Femininity**
4.4 **Uncertainty Avoidance**
4.5 **Long-term Orientation**
4.6 **Indulgence and Restraint**
4.7 **Country scores on Hofstede's Six Dimensions of Culture**
4.8 **Assignments**

In this chapter we will introduce more basic assumptions using the Dimensions of Culture by the Dutch researcher Geert Hofstede. We will relate these to the basic assumptions from the previous chapters as well.

In the second half of the 20th century, Geert Hofstede (1991) carried out research about values, among managers at the multinational IBM, in more than 50 countries. Despite the respondents' difference in nationalities, they shared a similar professional culture and a similar corporate culture – IBM culture. So you would expect them to answer the questions similarly. There appeared to be, however, huge differences. The source of these differences had to be the impact of their national cultures. Hofstede identified four areas, and later six areas in which cultures differ. He called them the Six Dimensions of Culture. A dimension is an angle from which you can compare a culture to other cultures.

1. Power Distance Index, 2. Masculinity versus Femininity, 3. Individualism and Collectivism, 4. Uncertainty Avoidance, 5. Confucian Dynamism or Long Term Orientation, and 6. Indulgence and Restraint.

Countries could score from 1 to 100 on each dimension. Some even score above 100 because of statistical procedures. Later Hofstede had the five dimension scores calculated for countries that were not included in his original IBM study. The newest, sixth dimension has not been added (yet). You will find all these countries and their scores in a table in 4.7.

We will now introduce each dimension.

4.1 Power Distance

Power distance explains why we assume that it is normal that power is distributed equally in our families, at school or at work. Or just the opposite, why we assume that it shouldn't be equal. In Hofstede's words, "it is the degree in which the less powerful members of an organization accept that power is distributed unequally." (1991).

Which countries are low in power distance? Netherlands, to start with, that's where this book was first written. Parents treat their children as equals in the Netherlands. Children are allowed to have an opinion; they may disagree with their parents. In class, you don't have to say, "Excuse me, may I ask a question please?" You may just raise your hand and ask (often without even raising your hand). Your opinion is valued in class. At work you don't have to wait for your supervisor to give you orders. You can just go ahead and take initiative.

Other low power distance countries are the Scandinavian countries, Germany and the German speaking countries, Great Britain and English-speaking countries such as the USA, Australia, and New Zealand. Israel is also low power distance.

Which countries are high in power distance? Just across the Dutch border, in Belgium, power distance is already a lot higher than in the Netherlands. Belgian students studying at Dutch universities are shocked at the ease with which Dutch students talk back at their lecturers in class, argue about their course assignments or negotiate for later assignment deadline dates. One Belgian student said, "I was speechless for the first 6 months of my studies! I was so embarrassed by my classmates' rudeness. But the lecturer didn't seem to have a problem with it. Her only problem was me – why didn't I participate in class discussions?"

In high power distance countries, people accept it that their superiors - meaning parents, teachers, bosses, or people older than you - have more power. Period. You don't argue with your parents. And you don't answer back in class for the sake of airing your opinion. However, it doesn't mean you can't give your opinion. You can, but in a very respectful, and sometimes indirect way.

Countries in Asia, West Africa, Latin America and Eastern Europe are very high in power distance. Latin European countries such as France, Central European countries like Poland and Czech Republic; and East African countries are between medium and high in power distance, thus relatively higher than the Netherlands. There are a few exceptions. Slovakia, which is in Central Europe, is very high, and Costa Rica, which is in Latin America is low in power distance.

For the multi-cultural Netherlands, students with an Antillean, Indonesian, Moroccan, Surinam or Turkish background, depending on how long they've been in Holland, are used to high power distance at home and low power distance at school. Sometimes it can be hard to find the right balance of being frank with your superiors without being rude.

Case 4.1 Ekaterina lacks initiative......

Illustration 4.1.

Ekaterina is a Ukrainian student at a university of applied sciences in the Netherlands. She is a top-student, with very high marks for all her subjects and projects. Ekaterina is now on an internship at an electrical engineering company in Delft, Netherlands. Her lecturer and internship supervisor, Gerard, pays the company a visit, and talks to Ekaterina's company supervisor and with Ekaterina.

The company supervisor, Mark, complains that Ekaterina lacks initiative. "She doesn't do anything!" Mark points out. "She's lazy, insecure. I have to tell her everything." Gerard listens in disbelief. Ekaterina? His top student, lazy? Ekaterina is in tears. "Yes, I wait for instructions. But everything I am instructed to do, I have done much faster and better that the other interns. I can't by-pass Mark, and start doing other things without consultation." (And she thinks, I'm calling in sick tomorrow.)

Questions for discussion

- What are the cultural factors causing this internship conflict?
- What are the scores for the Ukraine and for the Netherlands on power distance?
- How would you advise Ekaterina to go about the remaining period of her internship?
- How would you advice Mark, the company supervisor, on intercultural sensitivity?

Example

In Indonesia, instead of different words for brother and sister, there is a separate word for all older siblings, *kakak*, and all younger siblings, *adik*, distinguishing their rank in the family "line of command". You look up to your *kakak*, follow their advice and treat them with respect. You protect your *adik*, coach and care for them almost like another parent.

In some parts of Indonesia there are even two hierarchically different words for aunt, one for your father or mother's older sister, and another for an aunt who is their younger sister. The same counts for uncles.

4.2   Individualism

In an individualistic society, the ties between individuals are loose. You are mainly responsible for yourself, and for your direct, nuclear family.

In collective societies, people are part of close groups since birth. You are responsible for your group. The groups provide protection in return for unconditional loyalty.

What does this mean in terms of the collective programming of the human mind discussed in chapter 1?

In individualistic cultures, children grow up in small nuclear families, with one or both parents and one or two brothers or sisters. Grandparents, aunts, uncles and cousins live at a distance, and contact with them is not on a regular basis. So you are on your own. You learn to be "I"-oriented. And the aim of individualistic upbringing is to make you independent. In fact, independence is one of the highest individualistic virtues. Parents are proud of their children's independence, from being able to tie your shoelaces when you were three, to earning your own money doing newspaper rounds at age thirteen. It is not unusual for young people to leave their parents' house when they are eighteen or twenty.

Speaking your mind. That's another great individualistic virtue. It means you are honest and open. Even if you have to confront others, and if they too are good individualists, they have learned to take criticism as nothing personal, and do something constructive with it. People in individualist cultures obviously prefer a direct, low context communication.

In collective cultures children grow up in large families, sometimes in extended families, including grandparents or other family members. You are rarely alone. Children automatically learn to be "we"-oriented, and your identity is in the group identity. The aim of collective upbringing is to help you become a responsible member of your group. To be "interdependent" and to care for other group members are great virtues. Group, meaning all your social networks – family, friends, neighbourhood, hometown, classmates, fellow students at university, and colleagues.

Keeping harmony with the people you live, work and study with is another virtue in collective cultures. After all, if you're never alone, you can't risk getting into confrontations. Speaking your mind is not such a virtue, while criticizing and confronting is seen as downright rude. Even saying "no" is such confrontation, that people try to soften it with a kind of "yes" (see case 4.2.c).

Does that mean people never say no, or never criticize in collective cultures? They do, but in a subtle way, without hurting feelings. Without stepping on egos. Without making anyone lose face. In intercultural communication we call this blurring, and we will illustrate this in case 4.2.a. Characteristic for collective cultures is that they prefer high context communication.

Which countries are individualistic and which ones collective? Most individual cultures are in North America (Canada and USA), Australia and in North and Western Europe, followed closely by Central Europe. Netherlands – you guessed it right – is an individualist culture. Collective cultures are most of the countries in Asia, Africa, Latin America, the Middle East and Eastern Europe.

Intercultural sensitivity

Case 4.2.a Blurring

Illustration 4.2.

In many collective cultures, you have to maintain harmony in the group. It is not considered professional to criticize directly, and cause others to lose face. It is professional to do this indirectly by blurring. Here are three examples of blurring: blurring the message, blurring the sender or blurring the receiver.

Adriana, a lecturer from Argentina, a collective culture, teaches at a university of applied sciences in Breda. Adriana is not happy about two students who are talking, eating and drinking coffee during her lectures. Adriana would have liked to say "Stop talking, stop eating, or get out of my class." But she finds that too unprofessional and confrontational.

1. She blurs the message, by saying "Did you miss having breakfast? Would you like to take a break?" Students from collective cultures would take the hint and stop talking immediately. Not only that. They would admire Adriana's tact.

2. She could also blur the sender by not criticizing the students directly, but by asking the students' coaches, to talk to them about their behaviour in class.
3. She could blur the receiver by not picking on the two students directly, but by addressing the class as a whole about the disturbance of talking and eating in class in general. "Shall we all agree not to disturb the lectures with talking, eating and drinking?"

Question for discussion If you were a student in Adriana's class, how would you interpret her blurred message 1, 2 and 3?

Class discussion 4.2.b: for and against discussion on plagiarism

In individual societies, great value is placed on individual performance, privacy and originality. So at school and university, fraud and plagiarism are severely punished. Put yourself in the shoes of people from collectivist cultures. (For clarity, fraud and plagiarism are also forbidden there). Collectivist societies value interdependence, supporting group members and sharing. An idea doesn't belong to one person but is shared by the group who nurtured the creator of that idea. In this light, using or borrowing each other's intellectual property has a different meaning than pure plagiarism.

1. Split your class into two groups for a 10-minute discussion (5-minute preparation, 5-minute discussion). One group will prepare an individualist, hard policy against plagiarism. The second group is also against plagiarism, but will hold a more lenient stand towards it, from a collective, sharing point of view.
2. For and against discussions are a popular didactical form in individualist cultures. They are too confrontational for collectivist societies to be comfortable with. Now repeat your discussion on plagiarism, but rather than being confrontational, exercise tact, indirectness and blurring. You need to get your message across without hurting feelings or making anyone lose face! (5-minute preparation, 5-minute discussion)
3. 5-minute buzz group feedback Talk to the person next to you and evaluate both discussions.
    - What did you think, feel and do during the confrontational discussion?
    - What did you think, feel and do during the indirect, blurred one?

Case 4.2.c Tip 6. "Yes" means "Yes". That means you've made an agreement

Illustration 4.3.

If you ask a Dutch person something and he says "yes", then you have an agreement. You might say "yes" just to be polite, or to mean "yes, I heard you". Or just to avoid an argument or conflict.

For a Dutch person "yes" means you've made an agreement. Dutch people think it is terrible when foreigners say "yes" when they don't agree. Dutch people will usually keep their appointments, even if it's in their disadvantage. "Ali, can you come at 9 o'clock tomorrow?" "Yes" "Okay, agreed." Questions: Is this a clear appointment for Ali? For the Dutchman?

From Doe maar gewoon. 99 Tips voor het omgaan met Nederlanders by Hans Kaldenbach, 2004. Illustration by Carlos Nunez.

4.3 Masculinity and Femininity

Masculine and feminine are words from terminology that relates to social and cultural behaviour that is associated with men or with women. That is in contrast to the words male and female which relate to biological differences.

A masculine society is one where assertiveness, achievement and success are important values. According to Hofstede in masculine societies the emotional gender-roles are strictly divided. Men are expected to be assertive, tough and aim at material success, while women are expected to be modest, tender and oriented towards quality of life. We, however, notice in our own studies and research, that in many masculine societies, men as well as women are assertive and competitive. In different fields, perhaps, but competitive none the less.

Children in masculine societies learn that it is good to be the best. At school the students with the highest marks are admired, and are highly popular. People try hard to be "top of the class". Report cards don't only list the subjects and your marks, but often also your class rank. Number 1 in a class of 30 or number 20 in a class of 25. Students learn to like this. Teachers aim their lessons at the best students. When applying for jobs, you would write impressive CV's, exaggerating, and upgrading reality as much as you can. Whether at work, in your study or in private life, in masculine societies, men and women are concerned with everything in superlative form: who drives the flashiest car, who has the most expensive laptop, who wears the latest fashion.

In feminine societies, the emotional gender roles often overlap. Men as well as women are expected to be modest, tender and oriented towards quality-of-life.' just act normal' as they say in Dutch is a typical reflection of femininity in Dutch society.

In feminine societies children learn to be caring. At school, of course you learn to do your best, but that does not mean just competing for the best marks, but also being well balanced as a person, sociable and caring for other classmates. Students with the best marks are not necessarily the most popular. Teachers aim their lessons at the average students. And students aim for average marks, so they have enough time for a well-balanced social life. Does that mean nobody has expensive cars or flashy clothes in feminine cultures? They do. But they will often play it down, by saying, "The car was a bit expensive, but it's for the children's safety". About nice looking clothes: "Oh, I got them on sale." When applying for jobs, people write short, modest CV's. At work, you find quite a lot of men working in professions that used to be in women's domains like nurse, kindergarten teacher and stay-at-home-dad.

In fact, Geert Hofstede himself is a perfect example of feminine-culture-modesty. World famous, and in the list of top ten most frequently quoted writers in the world! Yet he remains very modest. We had the privilege of meeting Geert Hofstede at a congress for Intercultural Education, Training and Research. While other keynote speakers stayed together in special areas designated for the VIP's, Geert Hofstede sat with the regular congress participants, spoke softly, and made time to listen to others.

Where are the masculine cultures? Slovakia, Japan, Hungary, Austria and Venezuela are the five most masculine countries. USA and Australia are masculine. Other masculine countries in Europe are Britain, Ireland, Germany, Switzerland, Poland, Italy and Belgium (Wallonia).

Where are the feminine cultures? To start with, the Netherlands and the Scandinavian countries: Sweden, Norway, Denmark, Finland. Belgium (Flanders) is medium feminine.

Case 4.3

Illustration 4.4.

In several Scandinavian countries, the changing room for babies in public toilets may well be in the men's room rather than automatically in the ladies' room.

Question for discussion:

In what way does this reflect masculinity or femininity?

4.4 Uncertainty Avoidance

Uncertainty avoidance is the extent to which members of a culture learned to feel comfortable (or uncomfortable) in unstructured, unknown situations. Uncertainty avoidance is expressed in stress, and the need for predictability is expressed in the form of having strict formal and informal rules. This minimizes uncertain situations.

What are uncertain and unpredictable situations you may encounter as a student? Moving away from home, new regulations about exam registration, new internship requirements, going on internship for the first time, going on an exchange programme, a new lecturer, again a new project group, a vague assignment, the new Bachelor-Master system, the new curriculum. Uncertain situations at work? A new boss, a change in policy, mergers, acquisitions, new retirement policy, or dismissal.

In high uncertainty avoidance countries, children grow up surrounded by strict rules about what is and what is not allowed. What is clean and what is not. They learn at a very young age that uncertainty is a threat. At school and university in high uncertainty avoidance cultures, students like structured lessons, and clear assignments. Students get all stressed if they get assignments that they can interpret any way they want. Students want to know the correct answers, and their lecturers are supposed to give those right answers. At work in high uncertainty avoidance cultures, employees enjoy working for the same company for a long time. Safety and security are strong motivators. And there is a strong need for formal work regulations. Rules are not only the written rules. They also include unwritten, informal rules of behaviour, such as wearing the correct clothes, correct interaction – these are also rules.

Here are some of the countries that are high in uncertainty avoidance: A lot of countries in Latin America, for example, Argentina, Chile and Uruguay; In Europe it's Latin Europe, for example, France, Italy, Portugal, and Spain; The German speaking countries: Germany, Austria and Switzerland; Countries around the Mediterranean: Greece, Malta, Morocco and Turkey; Central Europe, for example, Poland, Czech Republic and Hungary; Eastern Europe; In Asia it's Japan, Korea and Taiwan.

As students, if you're working in a project group with students from high uncertainty avoidance countries, say from Germany or Argentina, do your best not to bend the rules. Work within clear structures, don't drive them up the wall with vague responses such as, "oh we'll do that sometime later". Be clear, "we'll do that on Monday". You will be rewarded with a highly motivated and effective project team.

In low uncertainty avoidance cultures (also called uncertainty accepting cultures), children grow up with flexible rules about what is and what is not allowed, what is good, clean and what is not. They also learn that uncertainty is normal, and that living life as it comes is also possible. At school and university, students in low uncertainty avoidance cultures enjoy lessons that are less structured, discussions, and assignments that you are free to interpret creatively in your own way. Lecturers don't have to explain everything, they can say "I don't know".

In low uncertainty avoidance countries, there are also people who have worked for the same company all their lives, but changing employers is quite normal. Achievement, appreciation, room for personal growth and social needs – these are motivating factors in low uncertainty avoidance countries. Of course there will also be rules at work, but not more than basic ones.

Which countries are low in uncertainty avoidance? With the exception of Japan, South Korea, Taiwan and Pakistan; all of Asia; Africa; the Anglo-Saxon countries. Scandinavian counties and the Netherlands score medium-low. These are countries where people can manage unpredictable situations well.

Case 4.4 Student-lecturer expectations

A Dutch lecturer wrote the following assignment for an international class consisting of Dutch and German students: Write a Cultural Profile for yourself according to Hofstede's Six Dimensions.

Most of the Dutch students went on and did the assignment. Half of the Dutch students did it right and passed. The other half did it all wrong, the lecturer told them to do it again. Some tried to negotiate and bargain for a passing mark, but finally they just did it again and then passed. Most of the German students found the assignment unclear. They asked, "How many pages should it be? Do you want us to explain the theory? Should it be practical too? When should we hand it in? What are the sanctions if we hand it in late? How do you want it?" In short, they wanted to make sure they knew how to do it, before they started, so they would make no mistakes. The lecturer got all irritated by the German students' questions. The German students lost respect for the lecturer's lack of responsibility for sending students off to do an assignment that had no structure, no explanation and no formal guidelines.

Discussion:

a. How does the above case reflect the difference in uncertainty avoidance?
b. Help the teacher and students in the case above. Rewrite the assignment description above in such a way that it leaves no room for misunderstanding, no unknown situations.
c. How will your rewritten assignment description benefit the German students?
d. How will it benefit the Dutch students? Would the rate of failure drop?
e. How would it benefit the lecturer?

Illustration 4.5.

4.5 Long-Term Orientation

Countries high on long-term orientation value thrift and perseverance. Their culture programmes you to value overcoming huge obstacles with time, strength and perseverance. (Hofstede & Hofstede, 2005: 211).

We will be very brief on this dimension, because the scores are available for only 23 countries. After a few years, more country scores became available through replication. Furthermore, the scores on this fifth dimension are not based on Hofstede's original IBM values research, but on the Chinese Values Survey (CVS) conducted

Intercultural sensitivity

by Michael Harris Bond, a Canadian professor who worked with Hofstede at the University of Hong Kong in the late 1980s. The CVS respondents were 100 students from each of the 23 countries in the research.

In long-term oriented countries, parents teach children that perseverance leads to results. They learn to be frugal with money. At school, students work hard, because that will result in great future success. If you fail it is because you haven't worked hard enough. And failure leads to loss of face. At work, self-discipline and responsibility are highly valued, and free time seems to get a lower priority. When it comes to investment, people think of returns in ten years.

Where are the long-term oriented countries? As shown in the end-of-chapter list, countries in East Asia: China, Hong Kong, Taiwan, Japan, Vietnam and South Korea. Followed closely by India, Thailand and Singapore. Brazil, with its important Japanese ethnic minority, also scores high in long-term orientation.

Medium. The Netherlands, has medium scores (44) for long-term orientation, and occupies a medium-high 13th rank. Several other European countries such as Hungary, Denmark, Norway, Ireland, Finland and Switzerland have medium scores.

In short-term oriented countries, children learn to achieve fast results with short efforts. They also learn to save money. But the social pressure to spend the money is great. At school students also work hard, but success and failure are often seen as results of luck and chance. At work people value freedom, rights, success and self-expression. Free time is very important. When it comes to investment, you think of returns in a year.

Illustration 4.6.

Where are the short-term oriented countries? As shown in the table, the Anglo-Saxon countries: Canada, Great Britain, the United States, New Zealand and Australia. Two African countries: Nigeria en Zimbabwe. Two Asian: Pakistan and the Philippines. Several Central European countries and Germany.

4.6 Indulgence and Restraint

This dimension was created in close cooperation with the Bulgarian interculturalist, Michael Minkov, who invested 10 years in researching the World Values Survey (WVS). WVS is an academic project including the social, cultural, religious, and political values of 93 countries. Minkov distinguished three dimensions, one of which was Indulgence versus Restraint.

In 2010, Michael Minkov, Geert Hofstede and Gert-Jan Hofstede published their 6th dimension.

According to Hofstede, Indulgence stands for "a society that allows relatively free gratification of basic and natural human drives related to enjoying life and having fun". While Restraint stands for "a society that suppresses gratification of needs and regulates it by means of strict social norms." (Hofstede, Hofstede and Minkov, 2010)

In indulgent societies, it is fairly easy to give in to pleasure, such as enjoying leisure time, being with friends, spending money, and romantic relations. High scores on Indulgence can predict high levels of feeling happy, family size and high participation in sports. (G. Hofstede, SIETAR-Netherlands Workshop, 2010)

In restraint cultures, the norm is just the opposite. We see societies where pleasure is controlled. A culture where people find it more difficult to enjoy life. Restraint correlates with pessimism in society, with health problems, saving money, low need for freedom of speech and with relatively high presence of police in society. (G. Hofstede, SIETAR-Netherlands Workshop 2010)

4.7 Country scores on Hofstede's Six Dimensions of Culture

	PDI Power distance	IDV Individualism	MAS Masculinity	UAI Uncertainty Av.	LTO Long term or.
Arab World **	80	38	52	68	
Argentina	49	46	56	86	
Australia	36	90	61	51	31
Austria	11	55	79	70	
Bangladesh *	80	20	55	60	40
Belgium	65	75	54	94	
Brazil	69	38	49	76	65
Bulgaria *	70	30	40	85	
Canada	39	80	52	48	23
Chile	63	23	28	86	
China *	80	20	66	30	118
Colombia	67	13	64	80	
Costa Rica	35	15	21	86	
Czech Republic *	57	58	57	74	13
Denmark	18	74	16	23	
East Africa **	64	27	41	52	25
Ecuador	78	8	63	67	
El Salvador	66	19	40	94	
Estonia *	40	60	30	60	
Finland	33	63	26	59	
France	68	71	43	86	
Germany	35	67	66	65	31
Greece	60	35	57	112	
Guatemala	95	6	37	101	
Hong Kong	68	25	57	29	96
Hungary *	46	80	88	82	50
India	77	48	56	40	61
Indonesia	78	14	46	48	
Iran	58	41	43	59	
Ireland	28	70	68	35	
Israel	13	54	47	81	
Italy	50	76	70	75	
Jamaica	45	39	68	13	
Japan	54	46	95	92	80
Luxembourg *	40	60	50	70	
Malaysia	104	26	50	36	
Malta *	56	59	47	96	
Mexico	81	30	69	82	

CHAPTER 4 Working with Hofstede's 6 Dimensions of Culture

	PDI Power distance	IDV Individualism	MAS Masculinity	UAI Uncertainty Av.	LTO Long term or.
Morocco *	70	46	53	68	
Netherlands	38	80	14	53	44
New Zealand	22	79	58	49	30
Norway	31	69	8	50	20
Pakistan	55	14	50	70	0
Panama	95	11	44	86	
Peru	64	16	42	87	
Philippines	94	32	64	44	19
Poland *	68	60	64	93	32
Portugal	63	27	31	104	
Romania *	90	30	42	90	
Russia *	93	39	36	95	
Singapore	74	20	48	8	48
Slovakia *	104	52	110	51	38
South Africa	49	65	63	49	
South Korea	60	18	39	85	75
Spain	57	51	42	86	
Surinam *	85	47	37	92	
Sweden	31	71	5	29	33
Switzerland	34	68	70	58	
Taiwan	58	17	45	69	87
Thailand	64	20	34	64	56
Trinidad *	47	16	58	55	
Turkey	66	37	45	85	
United Kingdom	35	89	66	35	25
United States	40	91	62	46	29
Uruguay	61	36	38	100	
Venezuela	81	12	73	76	
Vietnam *	70	20	40	30	80
West Africa	77	20	46	54	16

* Estimated values
** Regional estimated values:
- 'Arab World' = Egypt, Iraq, Kuwait, Lebanon, Libya, Saudi Arabia, United Arab Emirates
- 'East Africa' = Ethiopia, Kenya, Tanzania, Zambia
- 'West Africa' = Ghana, Nigeria, Sierra Leone

Source: ITIM.

4.8 Assignments

4.8.1 Your Cultural Profile According to Hofstede

What are your basic assumptions according to Hofstede? Are you low or high in power distance, masculine or feminine? Mark an I for yourself, and a C for the norm in your country.

High or low in power distance
Low   High

Individual or collective
Individual   Collective

Masculine or feminine
Masculine   Feminine

High or low in uncertainty avoidance
High   Low

High or low in long-term orientation (Confucian dynamism)
High   Low

4.8.2 Assignment: The Curriculum Vitae

Work in pairs. You are a student applying for several internship opportunities abroad. There are two interesting internship opportunities: one at a company in Sweden, the other at a company in the United States.

1. Each of you writes a short CV to send to the Swedish company. Write it modestly so that it will be regarded well in a feminine country.
2. Read your partner's CV
3. Now prepare to rewrite it for the American company. Advise each other on what you should change to make it more suitable for a masculine, assertive, achievement-oriented culture as the USA. (Don't make things up, but practice saying the same things in more superlative terminology, using more powerful words. Be proud of yourself, and be proud to tell about your successes)
4. Write your new CV to send to the American company.

5 Cultural Synergy: Trompenaars' 7 Dimensions and Cultural Reconciliation

5.1 **Universalism and Particularism. Rules or Relationships?**
5.2 **Individualism and Communitarianism**
5.3 **Emotions: Neutral and Affective**
5.4 **Involvement: Specific and Diffuse**
5.5 **Status: Achieved and Ascribed**
5.6 **Time**
5.7 **Attitudes towards the Environment**
5.8 **Reconciliation: from Vicious Circle to Virtuous Circle**
5.9 **Three steps to Cultural Synergy**
5.10 **Assignments**

In the previous three chapters, we worked with three classical intercultural studies: Hall's 6 Key Concepts, Kluckhohn's 6 Variations in Value Orientations and Hofstede's 6 Dimensions. In this chapter, these and an impressive range of other academic studies are brought together in a very modern and dynamic approach by Trompenaars: the 7 Cultural Dimensions. The first 5 of these cultural dimensions are concerned with how we relate to our fellow humans, and are called: 1. Universalism - Particularism, 2. Individualism - Communitarianism, 3. Neutral-Affective, 4. Specific - Diffuse, and 5. Achievement - Ascription. The last two cultural dimensions relate to time and nature: 6. The Concept of Time and 7. Internal Control - External Control.

This chapter then continues with Fons Trompenaars and Charles Hampden Turner's amazing Cultural Reconciliation. Their vision raises people out of the *vicious circle* of cultural clashes up into the *virtuous circle* of Cultural Reconciliation, to discover the boundless opportunities of cultural advantage and cultural synergy.

This chapter ends with a practical 3-step approach in achieving the advantage of cultural synergy.

5.1 Universalism – Particularism. Rules or Relationships?

What guides us? Commitments to rules or commitments to relationships? How do we judge people's behaviour? According to Trompenaars:

Universalists judge people as admirable if they keep to standards and rules agreed on in their culture. This is a rule-based society. Rules are there for everyone and under all circumstances. No exceptions. His examples of universalist countries are the USA, Australia, and Northern European countries, for example the UK, Germany and the Netherlands.

Particularists judge people according to the relationships they have. Are they your friends? Is she your sister? Is he important to you? Then you have an obligation to keep, and protect the person. Even if rules and regulations say you should not. (Trompenaars, Hampden Turner 2008) After all, who says the rule makers are perfect? We find examples of particularist countries in Southern and Eastern Europe, Latin America, Africa and Asia.

CHAPTER 5 Cultural Synergy: Trompenaars' 7 Dimensions

Case 5.1 The Driver and the Pedestrian

Illustration 5.1.

Created by Stouffer and Toby in the 1950s, Trompenaars' work raised it to become the most talked-about case in Intercultural history! Test yourself.

Your close friend is driving a car at 70 kilometres an hour in a 30-kilometres-per-hour zone. He hits a pedestrian. You are in the passenger seat, and only witness. Nobody else saw anything. Your friend's lawyer says that if you testify under oath that your friend was driving 30 km per hour, it will save him from serious consequences.

Question: Does your friend have the right to ask you this?

a. Yes. My friend has **all the right** to expect me to testify for the lower speed
b. Yes. My friend has **some right** to expect me to testify for the lower speed.
c. No. My friend has **no right** to expect me to testify for the lower speed.

Stouffer & Toby in Trompenaars & Hampden Turner 2008.

Among the participants of Trompenaars' research, more than 90 % of the respondents from the USA, Northern Europe and Australia refused to testify for a lower speed to protect a friend.

While 79% of the Brazilians, less than 75% of the French and Japanese, and even less than 60 % from Russia, China and India refused to protect a friend. (They would probably give their friend a serious talking to in private!)

On doing business in BRIC countries – Brazil, Russia, India and China – Fons Trompenaars and Peter Woolliams explain *Universalist or rule-oriented countries* ... "probably better satisfy the desire for distributive justice, but they may become obsessed with rules and regulations - which explains why the United States has so many more lawyers than Japan does." *Particularist or relationship-oriented countries* ... "tend to resolve failure privately, through relationships. The Swiss, North Americans, and Australians are the most rule-oriented, with 70% to 80% of respondents believing that exceptions to rules should not be made to help friends. In the BRIC countries, by contrast, only 25% to 40% would put the rule above the person." (Trompenaars & Woolliams, 2011)

How to reconcile these differences in order to gain cultural advantage? It is possible. Take a look at case 5.8.a further on in this chapter.

5.2   Individualism and Communitarianism

Trompenaars describes his second cultural dimension as "the conflict between what each one of us wants as an individual and the interests of the group we belong to. With Individualism being a prime orientation to the self. And Communitarianism as a prime orientation to common goals and objectives." (Trompenaars & Hampden Turner, 2008). We refer you to Hofstede's dimension Individualism – Collectivism in chapter 4.

5.3   Emotions: Neutral and Affective

How much emotion can you express? Let's first ask ourselves: What are emotions? And how important are they at the workplace, in your study environment or in international business? Stephen Robbins describes emotions as "intense feelings that are directed at someone or something." Not to be confused with moods, which do not need an object or direction. He identifies 6 universal emotions in the following spectrum: happiness – surprise – fear – sadness – anger – disgust. Evolutionary psychologists argue that people must experience emotions. There is a purpose for them, it helps us solve problems and it is critical in rational decision-making. (Judge and Robbins, 2010)

And yet, emotions used to be ignored in management studies. It was banned from the workplace with the myth that it was irrational and that it interfered with productivity. Nothing is less true. All this showing of desired work-related emotion while suppressing the actually felt emotion leads to what Robbins calls *emotional dissonance*. This *emotional labour* results in high stress and a waste of energy and resources. Recognizing the honesty and value of emotions is an asset for succeeding at work or in study environments world wide!

So it is good that Trompenaars put emotions on the agenda with the cultural dimension: Neutral - Affective.

In *neutral cultures*, (or affectively neutral cultures), you do not communicate your emotions, but control them. In fact if you do show your emotions by accident, you would feel compelled to apologize or dash out of the room.

Are people from neutral cultures cold and insensitive? Are people from affective cultures irrational and over-acting? Not at all. Every group has its unwritten norms about how much feeling you can show in professional surroundings, and how much should be controlled. The members of these groups have been conditioned at a young age to learn the proper way of expressing emotions, as well as the proper place. There is nothing good or bad about expressing emotions or suppressing them.

In *affective cultures* it is normal to communicate your emotions and to receive an emotionally sensitive response in return. There is nothing unreasonable about that.

> **Case 5.3**
> During his workshops, Trompenaars asked participants how they would act if they felt upset about something at work. "Would you express your feelings openly?"
>
> The highest percentage of "No's – thus most neutral - were given by respondents from Poland, Japan and Ethiopia. While the least "No's – so most affective – were given by his respondents from Cuba, Spain, Oman, Egypt and Kuwait.

Can we make an affective - neutral map of the world, continent by continent? Or by linguistic area? Not quite. But we think this dimension is important enough to discuss its variations within each continent.

Respondents from Europe were scattered between neutral and affective; with respondents from Poland, Bulgaria and Austria being most neutral; the UK, Hungary, Nordic countries, Netherlands, Belgium, Greece and Germany being medium affective-neutral; while Italy, France, Ireland, Russia and Spain were most affective.

Asian respondents from Japan were most neutral in not showing emotions at work, followed closely by Hong Kong, China, Indonesia, India and Singapore. Thailand and Malaysia were medium affective-neutral, while the Philippines and Middle East were most affective.

African respondents ranged from very neutral Ethiopia; neutral Burkina Faso and Nigeria; to the very affective Egypt.

From the American continent, Canadian respondents were most neutral; the USA, Mexico and Brazil medium affective-neutral; while Argentina, Venezuela and Cuba were most affective.

Australia and New Zealand were neutral in their responses.

We often think of sadness as an emotion. But happiness is an emotion too. And so is anger. Note that in one culture showing sadness, let alone crying is absolutely not done. But in the same culture, people can be perfectly comfortable showing anger and expressing angry looks on their face. While in other cultures shedding a tear is normal, but they would never ever show anger in public.

5.4 Involvement: Specific and Diffuse

How far do we get involved?

In *Specific-oriented* cultures you deal with other people in specific areas of life and single levels of personality. You separate the task-relation you have with someone, and isolate it from other dealings with him or her.

In *Diffuse Cultures* you deal with other people diffusely: in multiple areas of your life and at several levels at the same time. (Trompenaars & Hampden Turner, 2008)

This may remind you of Hall's Low and High context cultures, but it is not the same.

CHAPTER **5** Cultural Synergy: Trompenaars' 7 Dimensions

Case 5.4.a

Alejandro is an assistant to the marketing manager of a large department store. He reports directly to his manager, Susana. At work, Susana is a person of authority. Should they meet outside work, say at the golf course or at a New Year's party, would Susana still have any authority over Alejandro?

In Specific-oriented cultures she would not. Her authority is specifically related and isolated to the work area. And at one personality level: as his manager.

In Diffuse cultures she would. Her authority at work extends diffusely on to multiple areas, including the golf course and at private parties.

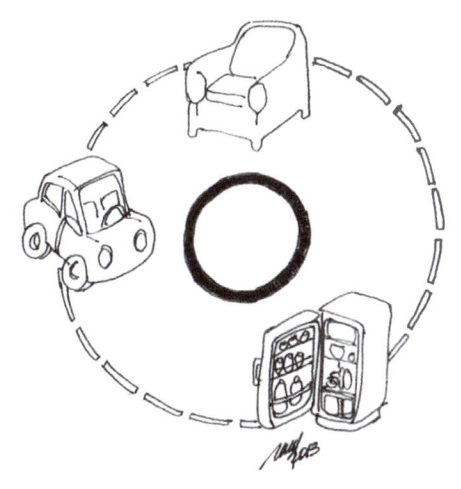

Illustration 5.2.1 Specific.

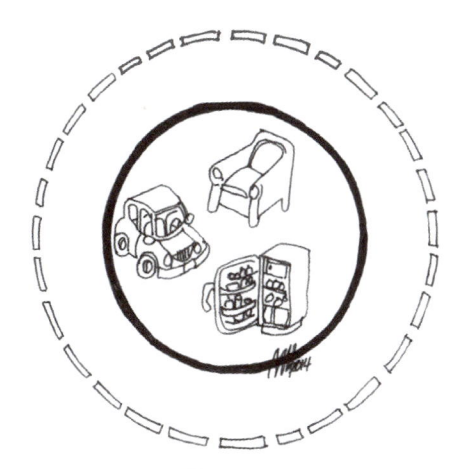

Illustration 5.2.2 Diffuse.

Case 5.4.b Lewin's American and German Space

Trompenaars refers to the work by the German-American psychologist Kurt Lewin, who illustrates the personality as a series of circles with life spaces and personality levels. Lewin contrasts American life spaces with German life spaces.

Americans have more public space, separated into specific sections: work, golf course, student association and so on. Colleagues who share those spaces are not necessarily good friends. They are not free to call you if the subject is not golf or student affairs. They have a small private space. The USA is an example of Trompenaars's Specific culture.

The German circle has a small public space and large private space. Here life spaces have a thick line, where it takes more time to be able to enter, and which requires the other person's permission. But once you are admitted to the private space, you are a friend, and admitted to all the other private spaces as well. This is an example of Diffuse culture.

What can go wrong when Specific meets Diffuse?

See case 5.4.b and the two types of life circles. Americans living in Germany often think of Germans as distant and difficult to make friends with, because they won't let you in their private lives. While Germans may think that Americans are friendly but superficial, because they will only let you into a small section of their public life.

Both ideas are stereotypes. They distort reality, and do great injustice to both the German and American culture. Understanding specific and diffuse spaces is one of the best ways of getting rid of these two stereotypes.

Do you remember the personal space exercise in chapter 3? Did you allow an acquaintance into your kitchen, refrigerator or car? A refrigerator can be semi public in one culture, while it is private in others. See case 5.4.c below.

Finally, specific and diffuse are relative terms. Compared to the USA, Germany and the Netherlands are diffuse. Compared to Indonesia, Germany and the Netherlands are more specific.

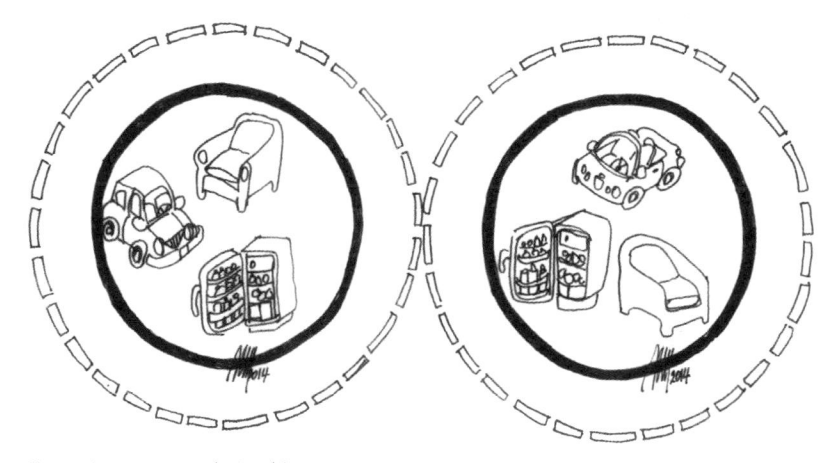

CHAPTER 5 Cultural Synergy: Trompenaars' 7 Dimensions

Illustration 5.2.3 No relationship.

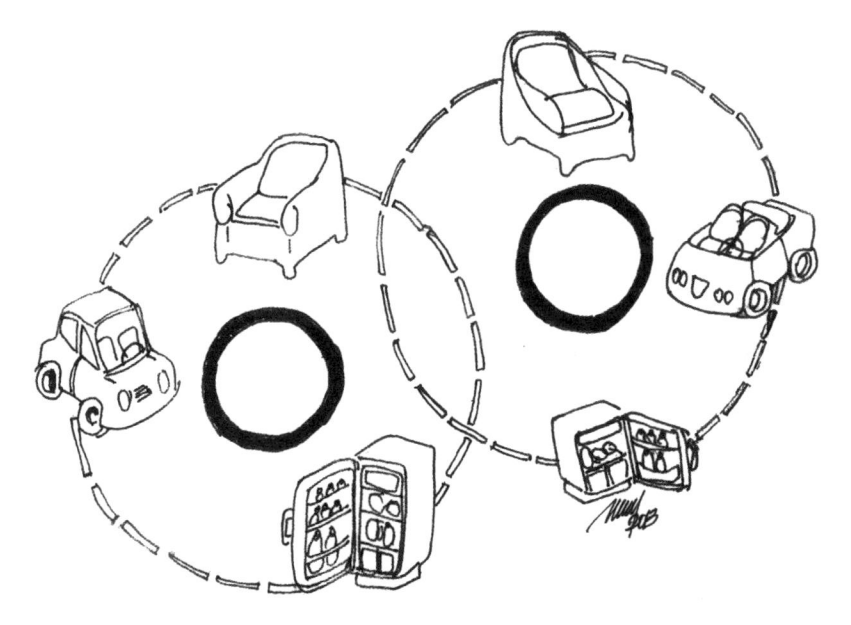

Illustration 5.2.4 Specific - Specific relationship.

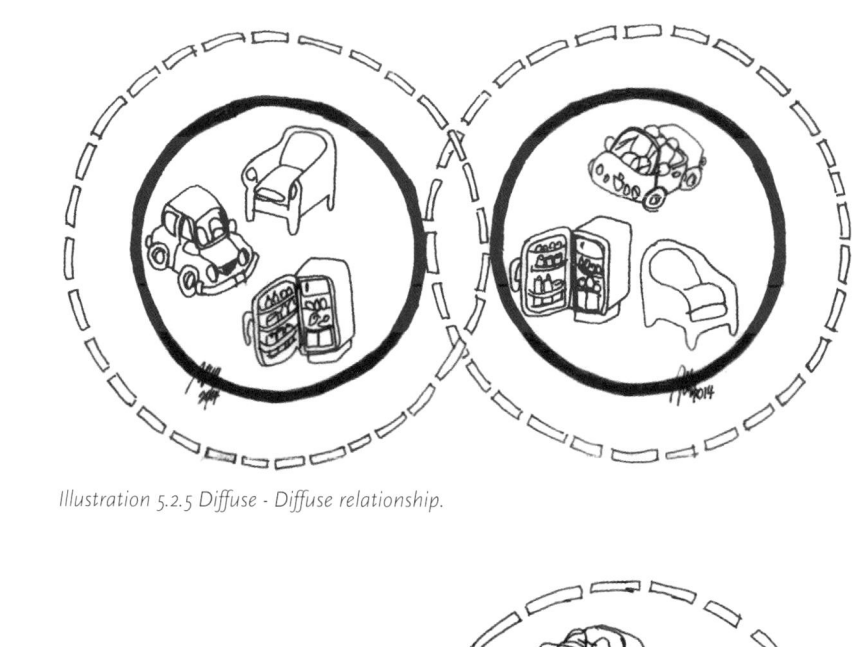

Illustration 5.2.5 Diffuse - Diffuse relationship.

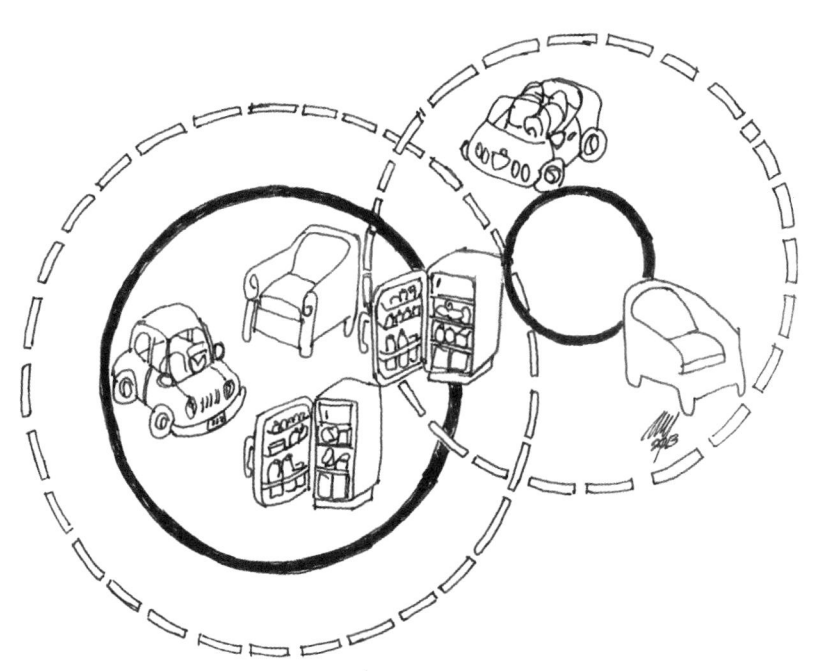

Illustration 5.2.6 Specific - Diffuse Encounter.

Case 5.4.c Close Encounters of the Diffuse Kind

Illustration 5.3.

Interculturalist Jacob Vossestein from the Netherlands, had invited an American colleague over for lunch at his mother's home in Utrecht. He was just about to ask what she wanted to drink, when he saw to his surprise, that she had already helped herself to a drink and a piece of cheese from his mother's fridge.

"How cheeky!" thought his mother. For Jacob's mother, the fridge was very private space. But for Jacob's colleague the fridge was semi public, and she felt she had been invited to use it.

Test yourself:

If you invite fellow students or colleagues over for drinks, is it okay with you, if they grab a drink from your fridge?

Could you elaborate on your answer using the terms Specific and Diffuse?

For more Specific and Diffuse practice, please turn to the assignments in 5.10: How can Dutch universities recruit more international students by applying Specific as well as Diffuse PR strategies?

5.5 Status: Achieved and Ascribed

How do you give status to people?

Achieved status is the high status you gain from what you have accomplished. What (not where) did you study ? Do you have a job? What is your job experience? What is your position? What have you achieved at work? In projects? What are you in charge of? Do you have a business? A lot of employees? Good income?

Ascribed status is the high status you gain because of whom or what you are associated with. Age, gender, social class, education, who you are related to and who you know. Who are your parents? Are you married? Is your spouse (or spouse's family) successful? Do you have children? How many? Do you have grandchildren? Land? Titles?

Case 5.5.a Samuel Thanks Jolene Through Wilhelmina

Illustration 5.4.

Samuel is a student from Ghana, at a Dutch university in Amsterdam. He was very touched by the efforts of a member of the International Office, Jolene, who had helped him succeed in his difficult search for student accommodation.

As soon as he signed the lease, he made an appointment with the Director of Studies at the university, Mrs. Wilhelmina Lind.

"Mrs. Lind", said Samuel, "May I ask you something? Could you please thank Jolene of the International Office for all her effort and dedication, in helping me find accommodation?"

"But you can also thank her yourself", said Wilhelmina, "I'm sure she will like that more"

"I thanked her", said Samuel, "But I am only a student. You are the director, and if you thank her, it will have more value."

Surprised, but delighted with this gift of cultural insight, Wilhelmina wrote Jolene a letter of appreciation.

Jolene was delighted too.

In Trompenaars' survey, respondents who scored high on achieved status came from the USA, Canada, Australia, UK, Germany and Scandinavian Countries.

For respondents from most other parts of the world, ascribed status was important.

Achieved or ascribed status – one does not always exclude the other. Cultures can be mainly achieved-status-oriented, with underlying ascribed status. The other way around as well.

Ascription and achievement status have their impact on everything we do. From how we introduce ourselves or write our CVs and resumes to how we express our opinions.

Some more examples on introductions which you may recognize yourself from encounters during holidays or staying abroad. Ask someone in the Netherlands or the USA who they are, and they will tell you what they *do*. Their name and their job.

Ask people from Brazil or India, and they will tell you who they *are*. Not just their names and professions, but also their family, relations and interests.

And if you are in Indonesia, see what happens if you only introduce yourself with your name and profession. You are bound to get the questions "Are you married? Do you have children? How many?" Obviously, if you are too young to be asked those questions, they will ask about your parents, brothers and sisters. It is not because Indonesians can't mind their own business. Indonesians are genuinely interested in you as a person.

In CVs aimed at employers in achieved-status cultures, you will probably highlight your own achievements – education, work experience, skills and hobbies – without mentioning the efforts of the people who helped you get there.

No matter what they teach you at Business Schools about CV and resume writing, CVs for ascribed-status employers may include more than that. If not in the CV itself, at least in the cover letter. Under work experience, you would name the important people under whose leadership you grew to the next promotion. During your studies, if you had a highly respected lecturer or a well-known professor, you can mention her or his name. If your mother was the one who inspired you in your professional development, don't hide it. If you are not comfortable putting it in your formal CV, do bring it up in the job interview.

Bear in mind though that managers from achieved-status cultures will be irritated by such CVs.

According to interculturalist Marta Carabba from Argentina, the best way to land a job interview in an ascribed-status country like Argentina, is through recommendations from friends and relations. The ones who recommended you have already updated your future employer on your qualifications. "So don't worry. Probably they won't even look at your CV during the interview. They know you are competent. But how are you as a person? How will you fit in the company, and the company culture?" (M. Carabba, Workshop Doing Business in Argentina, Royal Tropical Institute, Amsterdam 2002)

Achievement or ascription even influences the way we answer questions, whether we have to have the right answer on hand, or can admit that we don't know.

Case 5.5.b The André Laurent Question
Frequently quoted French interculturalist and professor at INSEAD, André Laurent, asked a famous question in a survey among international professionals.

Do you agree with this statement?

Chapter 5 Cultural Synergy: Trompenaars' 7 Dimensions

> *Managers must have the right answers to most questions asked by their subordinates.*

These are the percentages of the respondents who agreed:

Japan	78
China	74
Indonesia	73
Italy	66
France	53
Germany	46
United Kingdom	27
United States	18
Netherlands	17
Sweden	10

Source: André Laurent, SIETAR Poitiers, 1997; and as reported in N. Adler, 2002.

5.6 Time

Here again, we will refer you to chapters 2 and 3 of this book, Hall's Key Concepts and Kluckhohn's Values.

Trompenaars' 6th dimension is Time. Sequential and synchronic time as well as past-present-future orientation.

Sequential time refers to cultures where it is the norm to do one thing at a time, in a linear way, similar to Hall's monochronic time.

In *Synchronic* time people engage in several activities at the same time, as in Hall's polychronic Time.

Trompenaars also refers to the Kluckhohn-Strodtbeck studies which identify three time orientations: Past, Present or Future.

5.7 Attitudes towards the Environment

How do we relate to nature? Do we succeed in our business and daily lives by controlling nature and our daily problems? Or by going along with it?

Referring to the studies by Rotter on Internal Locus of Control and External Locus of Control, Trompenaars distinguishes two cultural types: Internal Control and External Control.

In historical perspective, *Internal Control* starts with humans surviving by acting against the natural elements such as floods, droughts and predators. If you control and eliminate the source of the natural problems, controlling becomes second nature. It goes on to professionals succeeding by taking control and imposing their will on the challenges they face in their career and organization.

External Control starts with humans surviving natural disasters by acting with the environment to make it less threatening, and more sustainable. Flexibility, creativity, and skills in riding nature's waves become second nature to you. It moves on to professionals who succeed by going along with the natural flow and direction in the organization.

No matter what preference people have for solving business and daily challenges: internal or external control, in global business you need both skills. So you *can* succeed with internal control by planning and shaping your whole life and career according to your will. And you *can* succeed with external control by listening and watching what is going on around you, and by re-directing yourself according to external forces. But by using both ways so as to complement each other, you can gain even more advantage.

5.8 Reconciliation: from Vicious Circle to Virtuous Circle

Awareness of cultural differences, awareness of our own cultural programming, and awareness that our cultural norms are not universal, are all starting points for reconciling cultural differences. Furthermore, like yin and yang, in every person the two extremes of each cultural dimension exist. You may be low context at work but high context when you start a conversation with someone you are in love with. Or empathize, as Trompenaars suggests, in the example of the car accident in case 5.1. As a universalist you can get close to a particularist if you imagine it was your father or daughter who was driving instead of your friend.

Trompenaars suggests **10 practical steps** in achieving cultural reconciliation.

1. Practice *Complementarity*, by realizing that cultural dimensions are not rigid, separate black and white blocks, but waves on a continuum, and that they are complementary.
2. *Use humour.*
3. *Map out a cultural space* along two axes as in case 5.8.a.

4. *Change cultural nouns to "ing verbs"* (present participle). So speak of universalizing – particularizing; individualizing – collectivizing or communing; specifying – diffusing; or using Hall's terms, monochronizing – polychronizing and so on. All at once, the rigid material nouns turn into fluid, dynamic processes. We think that is a fantastic idea.
5. *Language* achieves reconciliation by making it possible to handle two opposites in your mind and make them work. This is done using object-language (the real language we use to talk about things and objects, also about culture.) and meta-language (artificial language that linguists use to analyze sentences and the object-language itself). See case 5.8.b.
6. *Frames and Contexts.* Regarding the previous point on language, use meta level frames as context around the object level, to reconcile opposites. See case 5.8.b.
7. *Sequencing.* Instead of trying to juggle opposite extremes of a cultural dimension all at the same time, try sequencing them. You can go the opposite way and then correct yourself in order to reach your objective.
8. *Waving and cycling.* Rather than letting different values clash like billiard balls, Trompenaars suggests viewing them as waves and cycles, like the cycle of sleeping and waking.
The better I sleep, the more awake I am.
The better I stand up for my individual needs, the better I can care for my group, which in turn makes me a more content individual, and so on.
9. *Synergising and virtuous circling.* Instead of letting cultural opposites twist in vicious circles, Trompenaars proposes the virtuous circle - the synergistic upward leading circles. The Greek word 'synergos' means 'working together'. Synergy includes both extremes of the cultural values, and leads to harmony, mutual benefit, and to even better results than the sum of each individual contribution. 1+1=3, so to speak.
10. *The double helix* (double spiral), like the DNA model, is a metaphor for the 10 steps for reconciliation. The DNA double helix is a twisted ladder with 4 rungs running in opposite directions. The cultural double helix has 7 rungs – the 7 cultural dimensions, that can run in opposite directions. Yet the opposites are complementary, create humorous situations when they come together, the rungs on the ladder serve as cultural mapping space, and growth process. Each twist of the spiral expresses the language of growth in frames, sequenced in waves and cycles producing synergy.

Case 5.8.a Reconciling Universalism and Particularism

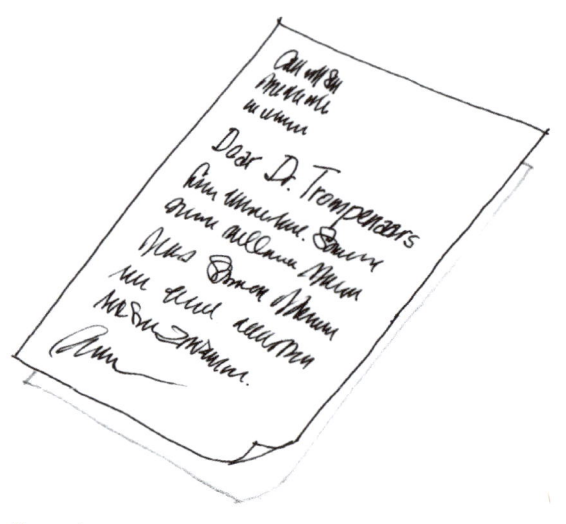

Illustration 5.5.

At a memorable SIETAR congress (Society for Intercultural Education Training and Research) in Poitiers, France, Fons Trompenaars told us about the intercultural training he had given to the senior managers and CEO of a large Korean multinational organization. Both Trompenaars and the Korean managers were pleased with their excellent personal as well as professional relationship.

Several months later, Trompenaars received a letter of appreciation from the CEO of the Korean multinational.

"We are very pleased to let you know that your book, 'Riding the Waves of Culture' has been successfully translated into Korean and it gives us big help for developing our organization's Globalization."

The CEO thanked him for letting them use his masterpiece within their organization.

"What?!" was the (UK) publishers' reaction when they heard about it. "They've translated it? They are using it? What about copyright?"

Any regular universalist would say, "Sue them!"

Then both parties lose. And it is the end of a good relationship.

A particularist might say "Thank you for the trouble of translating the book." But besides rescuing the dented relationship, what would you gain?

CHAPTER 5 Cultural Synergy: Trompenaars' 7 Dimensions

Go for a compromise? That would be ridiculous: split the difference, or "For you, my friend, I'll sue for half price!" Both ways a compromise ruins the relationship too.

While most managers would land in the vicious circle of blaming, Trompenaars showed us how he turned it into a virtuous circle and synergy.

He made his publishers aware of how much it would have cost them to translate the book into Korean themselves. Now it had been done for free, and the book was ready to be published in Korea.

He thanked the Korean CEO for having the book translated.

He asked if the CEO could recommend a good Korean publisher, who would publish "Riding the Waves of Culture" for the Korean market.

The CEO was delighted to. Not only that, he wrote a very positive foreword for the book, and since then Riding the Waves of Culture has been available in Korean!

A true masterpiece of cultural reconciliation and synergy (Source: Trompenaars, Workshop notes, SIETAR, Poitiers, France, 1997)

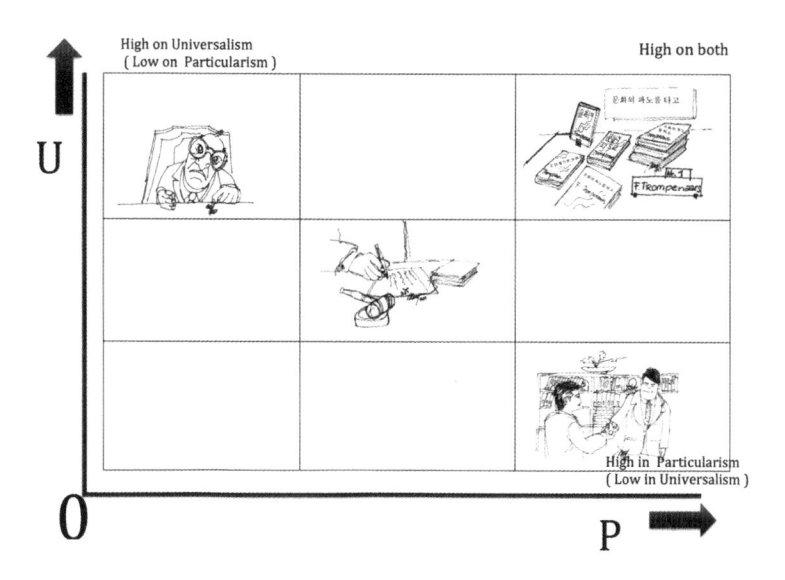

Illustration 5.6 Universalism-Particularism along two axes.

Case 5.8.b Language and Framing: Sustainable Development

To make this abstract concept clear, we will use the dilemma of sustainable development.

1. The world's resources are limited. The (past and) present generation is using them up.
2. The future generations have to have their share.

For years, people argued that you could not have both ideas in your mind, and be serious. The concept of sustainable development proves you can.

If you place the idea "The world's resources are limited" in the center of a square, and frame it with the idea "We want future generations to have their share", you are using meta-language and framing to reconcile two opposing ideas, and making them work.

The definition of sustainable development is:

"Development that meets the needs of the present without compromising the ability of future generations to meet their own needs" (Our Common Future / The Brundtland Report, 1987)

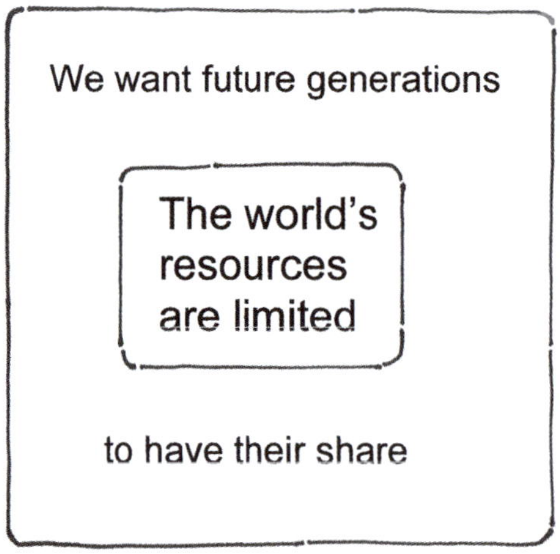

Illustration 5.7.

Raya Nunez, Cultural Perspectives in Sustainable Development, Working Paper, "5 Jaar na Rio, Locale Agenda 21", Utrecht 1997.

5.9 Three steps to Cultural Synergy

Besides the 10 steps to cultural reconciliation, we highly recommend a practical 3-step method to achieve cultural synergy (Adler, 2002). Readers of the previous editions of our book found it easy to use, because it is based on the 5 principles of conflict resolution. First we will briefly illustrate four other approaches to working with other cultures: *cultural avoidance, cultural dominance, cultural accommodation,* and *cultural compromise.* Finally, we will introduce the more innovative *culturally synergistic* approach in 3 steps.

In the assignments in section 5.10, you will practice achieving cultural synergy by using a real-life case from Dutch health care and a case from your own experience.

This table shows the five approaches to working with other cultures:

Table 5.1.

High on My Way · High on My Way and Their Way

Cultural Dominance				Cultural Synergy
		Cultural Compromise		
Cultural Avoidance				Cultural Accommodation

Low on My Way · High on Their Way
Low on Their Way

Case

A team of entrepreneurs from China, Egypt, Germany, India, Italy, the UK and USA are working on an innovative, and sustainable product, which will be launched world-wide, in November of the following year. Every month they meet in Rome, Italy. The meetings start on the first Monday morning of the month, at 10.00 a.m. Everyone is present on time, but the Egyptian, Indian and Italian team members are engaged in conversation, enquiring about the well being of each other's family. The others are eager to start the meeting. As usual, the meetings are only officially opened at 10.10. Ten minutes late.

(Adapted from Tricky, D. and Ewington, N.A.: A World of Difference, DVD)

Cultural Avoidance

In *cultural avoidance*, you avoid confrontation, and you don't impose your own cultural way of doing things in order to be professional. We know from chapters 2 and 4 that, what a monochronic assumes to be professional, differs from a polychronic's definition of professional.

The people who were seated on time are quite upset about the other team members' lateness. But they like their colleagues very much, and rather than getting everyone upset by complaining, they decide to ignore the waste of the first 10 minutes.

The other team members don't think they are late. They were present at 10.00. The exchange of news expressed their need to care about each other. They decide to ignore the fact that they were being rushed without having time to greet everyone. After all, they like their colleagues, and don't want to disappoint anyone by keeping them waiting, even for 10 minutes.

Nobody addresses the minor irritations of starting late or being rushed. This is cultural avoidance. It doesn't solve problems, just ignores them.

Cultural Dominance

In *cultural dominance*, you do what comes naturally from your own cultural background, and assume the others should adapt to you. In this approach, the chairman of the meeting, from the UK, would insist. No personal conversations during the meetings, and we start at 10.00 sharp. This would result in dissatisfaction among half the team members, and in loss of the exchange of information that the whole team could benefit from.

Cultural Accommodation

This is the opposite of above. Instead of doing what comes naturally in your own culture, you make a huge effort to do what the others do. This is what would happen if the Indian, Italian and Egyptian manager agreed not to have personal conversations with each other. It would make them very unhappy and take away the charm of the otherwise so serious business meetings. When it is exactly the diverse cultural background of the team that contributes to the international atmosphere and innovative results.

Cultural Compromise

If you culturally compromise, you do half of what comes naturally from your cultural background, and give up half. The others also keep half and give up half. A lot of people think that compromise is good. But compromise is still a loss of potential, since all parties are giving up half of what they could fully invest. In practice, cultural compromise would be to say "You can have 5 minutes of social conversation. And we'll start the meetings 5 minutes late." For the monochronics on the team, that is still late. For polychronics, why bother!

Cultural Synergy

In the *cultural synergistic approach,* you develop new ways of working. Forget about who has to adapt to whom. Forget who are the majority and minority. You value *all* cultures for making their unique contributions to making life and work more creative and dynamic. You consider all cultural styles of communication and behaviour as equally professional You recognize cultural differences as sources of innovation and growth.

Table 5.2. below shows you how to gain cultural synergy in 3 steps. Step 1 is to describe the situation from not one point of view, but all points of view. Step 2, you name the underlying basic assumptions of each culture involved. Step 3, you consider several alternative solutions that are not restricted to one culture, but transcend cultures. Look beyond cultural borders, grow beyond ordinary solutions, and reach the extraordinary.

Table 5.2 Creating Cultural Synergy.

Step 1 Describe the situation from all points of view

1.a. Tell the story from your point of view.
1.b. Tell it again speaking from the other person's point of view.

Step 2 Interpreting the cultures

2.a. What are the basic assumptions that explain your perspective and behaviour?
2.b. What are the basic assumptions that explain their perspective and behaviour?

Step 3 Increasing Cultural Creativity

Create new alternatives by leveraging the other cultures involved. Go beyond cultural borders.

Alternative A, Alternative B, Alternative C, etc.

- Select alternatives, always checking to see whether the solution fits the basic assumptions of all cultures involved.
- Implement the solution, but be sensitive to the feedback you get. Does it work? Correct it if it doesn't.

The result is cultural synergy.

Adapted from International Dimensions of Organizational Behavior by Nancy Adler, 2002, page 119.

5.10 Assignments

5.10.1 What is your cultural profile according to Trompenaars' 7 Cultural Dimensions?

5.10.2 Work in pairs. Read case 5.1 of the driver and the pedestrian

What is your answer? A, B or C?

What is your counterpart's answer? A, B or C?

Take 1 minute each to explain you answers to each other.

5.10.3 Specific and Diffuse

A university is trying to recruit more international students.

- Write 3 recruitment strategies that would appeal to students from specific cultures in the left circle. For example: 1. Show the list of subjects taught in each year of the study. Add 2 more.
- Write 3 strategies that would appeal to students and their parents from diffuse cultures in the right circle. For example: Show pictures of the professors who teach at the university.
- Add 2 more.
- Write 3 strategies that appeal to both cultures, below that.

   Specific
1. Show a list of subjects taught in each year
2.
3.

   Diffuse
1. Show pictures of the professors who teach at the university
2.
3.

5.10.4 Cultural Synergy Assignment for Health Care

Cultural clash at the family doctor's office

18-year-old Umar, from Turkey has just moved with her parents from Rotterdam to The Hague. Consequently, they need to find a family doctor in The Hague. Their new neighbours in The Hague recommended their own general practitioner, dr. Valstar, an elderly gentleman, and highly experienced doctor. His practice was just two blocks away. And he still had room for more patients. Umar's father didn't like the idea. He thought it wasn't appropriate for his wife and two daughters to be examined by a male doctor. It was okay for him. But he wanted a female doctor for the rest of his family.

Umar and her father are now at dr. Bos's office, their former family doctor in Rotterdam, to inform her of their move to The Hague. "To which doctor's office shall I send on your medical records?" asks dr. Bos. There is a silence. "Do you already have a new family doctor in the Hague?" Umar and her father both reply at once, "Yes." "No." "Well, yes," Umar explains, "doctor Valstar, but only for my father. Could you please recommend a doctor for my mother, my sister and myself? A woman."

"A man, a woman? What's the difference? A doctor is a doctor," insists dr. Bos, who is getting irritated, "It's their professionalism that counts!" Unable to send on the medical records properly, dr. Bos feels she has failed in transferring her patients to a colleague in The Hague professionally. Umar's father feels he has failed as well. He is convinced that according to his religion, male patients should be attended to by male doctors, and female patients by female doctors. He just wants the best for his wife and daughters. And he wants to explain this to dr. Bos, but in both cases he has failed (From Intercultural Resource by Safa Bouaazi, 2005).

Solve this case using the 3-step method in Table 5.2. Come to a culturally synergistic solution.

5.10.5 From your own experience

Work in pairs with another classmate. Describe an encounter you had with someone from another culture, an encounter that ended in a cultural misunderstanding. It could be an encounter with a fellow student, a lecturer, your landlord, or someone at work.

Then take the three steps to achieve cultural synergy.

Step 1. Tell your story. Then put yourself in the other person's shoes and tell it again from their point of view. Your classmate should help you see the other person's point.

Step 2. What are the basic assumptions of your culture? What are the basic assumptions of the other person's culture? Give new meaning to what happened.

Step 3. Select new alternatives, be very culturally creative and dare to go beyond cultural borders.

6 The Growth Process in Intercultural Sensitivity

6.1 Denial
6.2 Defence
6.3 Minimization
6.4 Acceptance
6.5 Adaptation
6.6 Integration / Intercultural Competence
6.7 Assignment

In chapter 1 we defined culture, and saw how culture determined the way we think, feel and act. And how we evaluate other people's behaviour according to our own cultural frame-of-reference. In chapters 2, 3 and 4 we became more aware of our own basic assumptions and our cultural "programming", as well as the basic assumptions of people with a different cultural frame-of-reference.

You are interculturally sensitive if you are able to look at different cultures from their cultural frame-of-reference, rather than from yours. You have cultural empathy. Not only in your thoughts, but you are really able to adjust your behaviour, because you want to. Although you know your limits, you are able to move between multiple frames-of- reference, without losing your identity, with great cultural flexibility and respect.

In this chapter we will be working with the intercultural sensitivity model of the American interculturalists Janet and Milton Bennett (2002). The development of intercultural sensitivity is not static, but a dynamic process in 6 stages, starting from *denial* ("There are no cultural differences. Just treat everyone as an individual"), *defence* ("Why should we learn their ways"), and *minimization*, on to *acceptance*, *adaptation* and *integration* or *intercultural competence*.

The first three stages take an ethnocentric approach to culture. That means we see our own culture as the point of reference. Evaluating other cultures through our own cultural glasses. The latter three are ethnorelative approaches to culture. You are able to place your own culture within the context of other cultures.

Intercultural sensitivity

Illustration 6.1 The sun rises and sets in our world. We are barely aware of other cultures, or cultural differences.

6.1 Denial

When we are in denial we think that cultures are all the same. Or we are not really aware of cultural differences. We lack the terminology for describing cultural differences.

People in denial say things like: "Oh, we're all the same." "There's a McDonalds everywhere." "We all drink Coke". They mean well, but they are in denial of cultural difference.

Metaphorically, illustration 6.1 is how we are when we are in denial.

6.1.1 Strategies for moving on from the denial stage

Do you have friends or neighbours who are in denial? The best way to help them move on is by making them aware of cultural differences in an entertaining way. Don't start right away with lectures about basic assumptions. That is too abstract. Start with visible artefacts of culture, the outer layer of Edgar Schein's cultural onion from chapter 1. You can organise exotic meals together, or potluck dinners. Invite people to wear their national dress and talk about their culture. Check the local museums for exhibitions on art, jewellery, or ceramics from other cultures. Celebrating feasts from other countries and cooking a meal together is a wonderful way of getting to know each other and new cultures.

Intercultural sensitivity

Illustration 6.2 Metaphorically, the sun stills rises and sets in our world and the rest of the world, if we notice them, are threats.

6.2 Defence

When we are in the *defence* stage, we are aware of cultural differences, but in a dualistic them-us way. As if there were only two cultures in the world. Ours and all those others. In the defence stage, other cultures are seen as threatening and inferior.

People in defence will say things as: "They don't even speak our language." "They refuse to shake hands." "They're taking away our jobs." "Democracy? They still have a long way to go…" "They should start by learning our language!"

If you ask someone in the defence stage to take intercultural sensitivity classes, they'll tell you: "Not me. They're the ones who need classes! Whose country is this anyway?"

Variation: Reversed Defence Janet and Milton Bennett's studies also show that there is such a thing as defence reversal (2002). That is to view other cultures as superior and your own as inferior. It is the same kind of them-us thinking, but reversed.

People in this phase will say things as: "I am so ashamed of our people". "I wish I could be one of them" "Intercultural sensitivity classes? No, not for me. But my compatriots, they could sure use some lessons!"

When we are in defence, our world looks a bit like illustration 6.2.

6.2.1 Strategies for moving on from the defence stage

To come out of the tight them-us polarisation, it is important for people in the defence phase to recognise and accept that besides cultural differences there are similarities as well. Research by Professor Shadid of Tilburg University in the Netherlands shows that in intercultural contacts, too much emphasis is placed on the differences between cultures, while overlooking the similarities. Miscommunication between different cultures are not so much caused by their real differences, but by the negative image they have of each other. (Shadid, 1994) Learning about other cultures, reading novels by writers from different cultures and watching foreign movies will open a whole new world for people in the defence phase. This is also an appropriate phase to start reading intercultural communication theories.

Intercultural sensitivity

Illustration 6.3 The sun still rises and sets in our little world. We know where they are, those other cultures. And if we can help them to become a little more like us, then it will be all right.

6.3 Minimization

When we are in *minimization* of cultural difference, we are aware of cultural differences, but mainly of superficial ones. We still see our own norms and values as universal, rather than cultural programming. And we still interpret other cultures through our own cultural glasses. Because of that, we will judge other people's behaviour according to what is right or wrong, good or bad according to our norms. We will want to change them. Or help them to change, so they'll be more like us. Then they'll be alright.

People in minimization often say: "They eat with chopstick, and we use fork-and-knife, but besides that, we're basically the same." "Shall we teach them how to hold their fork and knife?" "Shall we give them lessons on emancipation?" "Shall we give them language lessons?" "Going on internship to Finland? Oh, just be yourself and everything will be fine"

If you suggest "Intercultural sensitivity classes?" to someone in the minimization stage, they'll probably say, "All I need is a list of do's and don'ts."

Illustration 6.3 is what our world looks like when we are in minimization.

6.3.1 Strategies for moving on from the minimization stage

Awareness of our own culture, of our own cultural programming, is the most important lever for moving on from the minimisation phase, and making the huge shift out of the restricted ethnocentric vision into the dynamic world of culture-relativity. Now it is important to have the theoretical framework of culture, in order to place our own norms, values, and basic assumptions within a larger context and to realise that our own norms and values are not universal.

Intercultural sensitivity

Illustration 6.4 In our perception, the sun no longer shines over our little world, but on the whole world. We want to learn as much as possible about other cultures and also about our own culture.

6.4 Acceptance

When we are in the *acceptance* stage we are able to recognise and accept cultural differences in values and behaviour. In this phase we see cultural difference as a source of new ideas and solutions to problems. It is the beginning of cultural relativism.

What do you hear people say at this stage? "The more cultures, the more ideas!" "We're equal, but not the same." "Intercultural sensitivity classes? Sure! Lots of them."

When we are in acceptance, our world looks like illustration 6.4.

6.4.1 Strategies for moving on from the acceptance stage

When we are in this stage the most important thing to learn is cultural empathy. To put ourselves in the shoes of the person from another culture. To learn to look at another culture from that other culture's cultural programming. It's called "Cultural-Frame-of-Reference-Shifting". Role-play and simulation games, are effective training methods. Simply living, studying or working in another country are excellent ways of acquiring this cultural empathy. Lecturer mobility, international student exchange programmes and internships abroad are creating wonderful opportunities for cultural-frame-of-reference-shifting. Especially if we don't take the easy way out, by only meeting the international students' crowd, or staying confined to the expatriates' world. To gain this cultural empathy, we really need to mingle with the local culture and the local population, while we are abroad.

Illustration 6.5 Frame-of Reference-Shifting. In adaptation, we are able to place ourselves in the norms and values system of the other culture, and adjust our behaviour.

6.5 Adaptation

When we are in *adaptation*, we are able to evaluate another culture from the frame-of reference of the other culture. And we are able to adjust our behaviour appropriately. We are able to place ourselves in the norms-and-values system of the other culture. We are able to behave according to the other culture's norms-and-values system. What is the difference between adaptation and acceptance? Aren't they both culture relative? Acceptance is on the knowledge level. You know. Adaptation is on the knowledge and behaviour level. You know, you feel and you can behave in a culturally professional manner.

What do people in adaptation of difference say? "To solve this problem professionally, I am going to try a different strategy." "I always shake hands when I meet people, but she prefers not to. So I won't shake hands" "I don't usually shake hands, but it would hurt her feelings if I didn't. So I'll shake hands." "They are doing their best to learn my language. It's high time I try and learn their language too!" And yes, people in adaptation enjoy intercultural sensitivity training.

Our world looks like illustration 6.5 when we are in adaptation to cultural difference.

6.5.1 Strategies for developing even further when you are in adaptation

Keep practicing frame-of-reference shifting. Practice mentally putting yourself in the norms-and-values system of other cultures. Practice solving case studies with culturally relative trainers. See the adjustment of your behaviour as professionalism; you're doing it because you want to. Don't worry if the other parties adjust themselves less than you do. This is not a let's-see-who-adapts-more competition. It's about personal, cultural and professional growth. Travel. Learn new languages. Every language you learn opens up a whole new world, a world of opportunities.

Intercultural sensitivity

Illustration 6.6 In the Integration/Intercultural Competence stage, we are able to practice multiple frames-of-reference.

6.6 Integration / Intercultural Competence

In this stage we are able to practice multiple frames-of-reference, or bi-cultural frames-of-reference. Our cultural empathy makes us good intercultural mediators. You have a bi-cultural or intercultural identity, you know your limits and it doesn't confuse you.

People in integration often say: "My management skills have improved since I use multiple frames-of-reference". "I feel at home in many places".

In the integration / intercultural competence stage, our world looks like illustration 6.6.

Third Culture Kids (TCKs), children of mixed cultural marriages, or who grow up bi-lingual or tri-lingual, or grow up in different cultures, are able to acquire multiple frames-of-reference easily. As long as they are not forced by their social surroundings, to choose one culture they have to belong to. They can enjoy multiple cultural identities without having to make an identity statement. If your mother is Australian and your father is from Somalia, then you probably grew up bilingual and with different sets of norms and values, which both make sense to you. You've been practicing frame-of-reference-shifting ever since you were born. If your parents are Moroccan and you grew up in the Netherlands, same thing. You have multiple-frames-of-reference. Or bi-cultural frames of reference. If you have TCKs and ATCKs (Adult Third Culture Kids) at your school and in your organization, they are good resource persons, with their ease in frame-of reference-shifting.

On a final note, the growth in intercultural sensitivity is not a rigid, linear process. It is dynamic. It can evolve circularly, or in all directions. It might develop step by step, but it doesn't have to. All the stages may just as well develop simultaneously.

6.7 Assignment

Step 1. Time: 1 minute. Group Formation. Form three groups: Group 1 is in denial Group 2 is in defence Group 3 is in minimization.

Step 2. Time: 5 minutes. Role Play Preparation. Each group reads their role play instructions below, and prepares their role play.

Group 1 "The Staff Meeting"

Group 1 is at a university staff meeting. Agenda point 1 is to hire more international lecturers to work at the school, because they are supposed to bring in new ideas. How do people in denial act and speak in a meeting? You may overdo it. You have 5 minutes to prepare a 3-minute role play called *The Staff Meeting*. Group 2 will observe and recommend strategies for raising cultural sensitivity.

Group 2 "The Lunch Break"

Group 2 are employees in the canteen, having their lunch break. They are talking about the new immigrants working in the construction sector of their city (nobody else seems to be available for those jobs). Depending on your interests, you may replace construction sector with health care, agricultural or IT sector. How do people in defence think, act and feel? You may overdo it. You have 5 minutes to prepare a 3-minute role play called *The Lunch Break*. Group 3 will observe and recommend strategies for raising cultural sensitivity.

Group 3 "The Seaside Management Day"

Group 3 are university managers on a management day at a seaside congress hall. They are worried about the slow progress and high drop out rate of foreign students. They want to look into this problem and do something about it. How do people in minimization of difference think, act and feel? You may overdo it. You have 5 minutes to prepare a 3-minute role play, *The Seaside Management Day*. Group 1 will observe and recommend strategies for raising cultural sensitivity.

Step 3. Time: 10 minutes (3 x 3 minutes + 1 extra). Role Play First Round. Each group acts out their role play in no more than 3 minutes. Other groups watch.

Step 4. Time: 5 minutes. Intercultural Consultants Group Meetings. You are intercultural consultants. Recommend strategies for raising cultural sensitivity to groups 1, 2 and 3. Group 2. Hold a group meeting. What advice can you give group 1 to raise them out of the denial stage? Group 3. Hold a group meeting. What advice can you give group 2 to raise them out of the defence stage? Group 1. Hold a group meeting. What advice can you give group 3 to raise them out of the minimization stage?

Step 5. Time 9 minutes. (3x3 minutes) 3-Minute Intercultural Consultants' Advice. Group 2. Give your 3-minute advice to group 1 Group 3. Give your 3-minute advice to group 2 Group 1. Give your 3-minute advice to group 3

Step 6. Time 5 minutes. Role Play Preparation for the Second Round. You followed the intercultural consultants' recommended strategies. Now group 1 is in acceptance. Group 2 is in adaptation. Group 3 is in integration/ intercultural competence. Prepare to repeat the role play from step 2, but now in your new roles: acceptance, adaptation and integration/ intercultural competence

Step 7. Time 10 minutes (3x3 minutes + 1 extra). Role Play Second Round. Each group acts out their new role play in no more than 3 minutes.

Step 8. Time 5 minutes. Conclusion. Write down your conclusion. What did you learn from this exercise? What are the benefits of intercultural competence? Write down your conclusion.

7 Culture Shock While Studying Abroad

7.1 Culture Shock. What is it?
7.2 What are the Stages of Culture Shock?
7.3 Pre-Departure Stage
7.4 The Vacation Stage
7.5 The Angry Stage
7.6 Adjustment Stage and Strategies
7.7 Re-entry Shock
7.8 Assignments

7.1 Culture Shock. What is it?

Culture shock is a process of adjusting from living in a familiar, predictable environment to living in a country where everything is new. The landscape, climate, people, language, food, religion, holidays, and culture – everything is totally different, unpredictable and uncertain.

Anyone who moves to another country to live, work or study may expect to experience culture shock. Whether the move is permanent, as for immigrants, or temporary, as for expatriates and exchange students, knowing what to expect and recognising the symptoms, will help you manage culture shock.

In this chapter we will mainly look at culture shock from a student's experience. We will give examples of how students feel, so that you'll know what to expect. For strategies on how to deal with culture shock in your future international careers, we recommend reading N. Adler, International Dimensions of Organizational Behavior, the chapter on Professional Entry and Re-entry in particular.

7.2 What are the Stages of Culture Shock?

This process of culture shock already starts before you leave, with a feeling of stressful uncertainty. Right after arrival, a lot of people experience an exciting "vacation feeling". It is followed by a time of great emotional and physical distress. This is not a sign of weakness or failure. Just the reverse, it's a sign that the individual is struggling hard to learn the new culture. For some people the distress is so great that they decide to return home. But most people gradually learn new skills and adjust to the new culture, although the adjustment strategies and the how much time they need may differ greatly from person to person. Among the students we interviewed, Michiel's vacation stage lasted two or three months, Carolyne's was over in two weeks, while several other students reported falling into deep emotional stress, disorientation and intense homesickness after a few days.

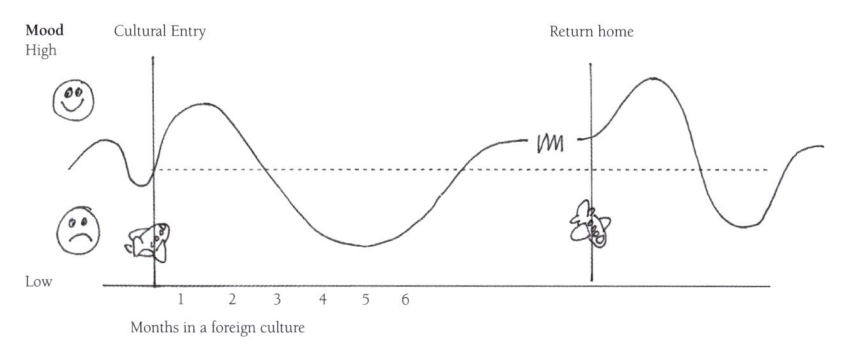

The Culture Shock and Re-entry Shock Curve
Months in a foreign culture

Culture Shock Stages: Pre-departure Vacation Stage Angry Stage Adjustment Re-entry Shock

Adapted from Adler, 2002:227.

The Culture Shock and Re-entry Shock Curve

[Graph: Mood (High/Low) vs. Months in a foreign culture (1–6), showing Cultural Entry and Return home points with a wave-like curve.]

Culture Shock Stages: Pre-departure   Vacation Stage   Angry Stage   Adjustment   Re-entry Shock

(Adapted from Adler, 2002:227)

Illustration 7.1 Culture Shock Curve.

Intercultural sensitivity

Case 7.2.a
This is how Carolyne Kiplagat, from Kenya, experienced Culture Shock while studying in the Netherlands.

"Everything in the beginning was like Wow! Everything in Holland is systematic. Everything is efficient. Especially the buses. It is very nice.

After some time, maybe two weeks, I noticed the people were not so friendly. You cannot talk to anyone. Everyone is busy. You cannot communicate. I felt like 'they don't care.' Even students. They mind their own business. I felt so homesick. I missed people you can just talk to. I missed my family. I missed my friends. Friends you have fun with. Friends who said 'Let's do this! Let's do that!' I missed that. I also missed the green nature, and the gardens. In Holland, I just saw cities, buildings, cars, bikes. And a lot of people in the cities. People who don't talk. I could not read the signs in the shops and on the streets, because I did not understand Dutch. And I felt completely lost.

I tried to figure out the meaning of the Dutch signs from German. Because I studied German at school, and Dutch has a lot of similarities with German. Now everything is okay. I have learned Dutch. I understand. It is a different society. People can be friendly even if they don't talk."

Illustration 7.2.

7.3 Pre-Departure Stage

Actually, culture shock already sets in before you even leave your country. As one Dutch student, Milou, said, "It was the most uncertain time of my life." (see case 7.3.b). Another Dutch student, Michiel, recalls this time as "chaotic and stressful". Pre-departure is a time full of uncertainty. Will you meet the requirements to leave? Will you be going to the country you want to go to? Will they send you somewhere else? It's a time of hard work and preparation. Living in uncertainty, depending on others to help you is a very stressful experience, especially if you are from an individual, dominating-over-nature-culture, and are used to getting things done yourself.

Case 7.3.a Milou's pre-departure stage

During her second year of study, Milou applied for an exchange programme to spend her third year of study abroad at a partner university in Florida, the US. There were only three places for exchange students, and thirty students wanted to go there. So imagine the competition and stress for Milou. "You had to pass all second year exams", said Milou, "Gather all that year's credit points, and write a very good letter of application with excellent recommendations. So I spent all my weekdays going to class and running from teacher to teacher, asking for letters of recommendation. All weekends I studied for the exams. My boyfriend was upset that I had so little time. When I heard the announcement that I was one of the three selected for the US, I was thrilled, but not for long. Booking the cheapest flight was the least of my worries. What was I going to do with my room? Cancel the rental contract, or sublet it? Was that allowed? Where would I leave all my stuff? In my mother's garage? No. She had finally gotten the building permit to turn the garage into the kitchen of her dreams. One box was all I could leave with her. The rest I left at my boyfriend's parents". With her ticket in hand, and one day before her flight, Milou's boyfriend actually begged, "Please don't go."

Illustration 7.3 "Please don't go...".

Case 7.3.b Michiel's pre-departure stage

I spent my third year of study as an exchange student in Barcelona.

Preparing for my year abroad was big chaos. I was still on internship till just a week before my departure. There was still a lot to arrange.

From the minute my school told me that there was a place for me at the UB, Universidad de Barcelona, everything went on automatic pilot. I realised that I was about to spend a whole year studying at one of Europe's most popular holiday destinations.

The most important things to arrange were finding an apartment, and filling out piles of forms. Insurance forms, Erasmus scholarship forms, Dutch study grant (IB-group) forms. Not to mention al the things I still needed to arrange for school – such as passing certain subjects and getting the right number of credits in order to fulfil the qualifications needed to go on a third year abroad programme. But all this stress, you forget it the minute the plane lands.

7.4 The Vacation Stage

You are abroad at last! The first few weeks or even months after arrival, most people are excited, positive and full of energy! You look around and can't believe your eyes or ears! New places, new people, shop windows full of stuff you've never seen. Food tastes exciting. The foreign language sounds exotic. Your language blunders are amusing. You move into your new room. Okay, the heater doesn't work, but wow, you're abroad, and this feels like a vacation.

Whether this vacation stage last a few months, a few weeks, or only one or two days depends on a lot of circumstances. Did you yourself want to go abroad? Or were you dragged along? Young people, who had to leave their friends behind and move abroad because of their parents' careers, seldom experience a vacation stage. In fact they feel miserable right from day one. But for students, this isn't the case. They do experience a few weeks or months of euphoria, and enjoy their new world as if it were a long vacation.

Case 7.4 Michiel's vacation stage

The first few days and weeks were like a vacation. Everything, really everything, was easier and better than in Holland. I tried to do as much as possible, because one year isn't that long. I embraced everything that had to do with Catalan and Spanish culture. I only at ate and drank typical Catalan or Spanish food and drinks. The Spanish girls were beautiful. I learned the language, went out a lot, made a lot of friends, and I was never at home.

7.5 The Angry Stage

After the first phase of euphoria comes disillusion. It's very, very tiring to think and speak in a foreign language all day, day after day. You try, but you can't say what you mean. You don't always understand what they say. And when they laugh about your accent, you feel a pain inside. It isn't funny anymore. The little in-crowd jokes that your new friends make in an attempt to make you feel included, you don't get them and you feel excluded. Again the pain creeps up your chest. You feel like an outsider. You long for the easy familiarity back home. How you yearn for your family. And you have to clench your jaws very tightly to hold back your emotions. The food is no longer exciting. You crave for food from home.

It's not just the language, or the food. All the new sound, sights, smells and uninterpretable cues around you, they're confusing, they're frustrating, they drive you to fury.

This is the stage, often referred to as culture shock. It can last several months or even years! For students on a year abroad, it's around three to six months. People in culture shock often feel they have failed in some way. They feel angry and insecure. They easily cry, easily lose their tempers. They idealise the situation back home. ("Traffic jams? We never had them in Holland.") They start hating the local culture, blame the local people for the frustrations, and go on and on complaining about minor little incidents. They wish they just could pack their bags and leave. Some people do. Most people, however, little by little crawl out of this deep valley of frustrations, and start learning new skills for living in the new country.

Case 7.5 Michiel's angry stage: Nothing works, blame the locals.....

After a while, the excitement wears off. Everything I liked so much about Barcelona? It all became a source of irritation, and I started hating it. It was winter. The sun was no longer as warm. Now I started discovering the bad habits of my flatmates. I had done my best to learn the language, but I still couldn't speak it well enough to follow a meaningful conversation. Suddenly I didn't like the food anymore. I didn't like the supermarkets. I didn't like the Spanish girls anymore. I didn't like them as much as the girls in Holland.

Then came the first round of exams. I had to take it easy. And I needed to rely on my newly made friends for support. Suddenly my new friends seemed so superficial compared to my friends in Holland. I secretly started missing Holland and missing Dutch things. This was in the 3rd or 4th month in Barcelona. I didn't want to go out. I didn't want to do anything.

The worst part was when Christmas came. I had made up my mind not to go home for Christmas. I said I wouldn't need this. And my new friends, the international students – they had gone home for Christmas. I was completely alone.

7.6 Adjustment Stage and Strategies

In this stage you have started to learn more about the new culture. From all the sounds, sights and smells around you, you can select what is meaningful, and learn to ignore what is not important. You no longer interpret what you see according to the basic assumptions of YOUR culture but of the new culture. You have developed a new circle of friends and support system.

Case 7.6 Michiel: Barcelona, Adjustment Stage

After about 5 or 6 months I began to feel better, more settled. I felt at ease. Now was the time that I wanted to go out again. I wanted to do as much as possible again. I knew it would soon be time to leave. From then on, everything was special and very nice to experience.

7.7 Re-entry Shock

Re-entry shock is the process of fitting back in your old familiar environment, after living, working or studying abroad: a reversed culture shock. You would think it was easier. But it's actually extremely difficult, because you don't expect it. Re-entry shock follows a similar pattern as culture shock. It's often shorter, but more intense.

We have extended the graph of the culture shock cycle at the beginning of this chapter, with a re-entry shock curve.

While people in our surroundings may sympathise with someone in culture shock, if we have re-entry shock, they say, "What? Culture shock in your own country? What a snob!"

At first you'll be overwhelmed with joy. Being back, seeing all the people you've missed, and eating the food you craved for while you were away. But not for long. Your stories about your experience abroad? No one seems to be interested. No one has time. They can't follow you. You've changed a lot and so have they. With all the new things you learned abroad, you feel cramped in your own town, at your old school, and fall into a deep disillusion of re-entry shock. A lot of students will start blaming the school. "This school is terrible. Everything was better at the school abroad." And if it were up to you, you'd hop on the first plane back to the country you just left.

20% of all international managers returning from abroad quit their jobs and fly straight back to where they came from. What a loss for the organisation. The figures for students are not known, but a large number of students want to quit their studies at this stage. We hope you won't.

When you return from your study abroad, or internship abroad, your experience is a huge asset. Not only for yourself, but also for your fellow students and for your school. Write about it in the school newsletter. Volunteer to speak at the Study-Abroad-Information-Days that your school is organising for students next year. They'll listen to your stories! Be a host to foreign exchange students studying at your university. After all, you are an intercultural expert!

Case 7.7 Michiel's re-entry shock

Okay, I had culture shock in Barcelona. But that was nothing. Coming back, that was the toughest part of my study-abroad-year. After all the cool experiences in Barcelona, it was so boring to just come home and do the same old things I used to do, and go on with my life like nothing had changed. The first day back at school was fun. The first time back at to my old discotheque too. Just for a while, it is all new again. A very short while. Then I felt completely out of place. With my old friends I had this "Okay,-if -you-knew-what-I-have-experienced" attitude.

I was glad to see my old friends again. But after a few days, I just wanted one thing: to head straight back to Barcelona. Once again, everything was better and faster in Barcelona. Here at home, everything was so normal. My room was the same. My school was the same. The friends around me were the same. In Barcelona I had gotten used to living with different people, making friends quickly, and living a fast-paced life in a completely different culture.

The first few months were so difficult. This time I wasn't struggling to learn a new culture. I was struggling to get used to my own culture.

I've been back for a year now. Looking back, my year studying abroad was a fantastic experience. I recommend it to everyone.

Illustration 7.4 "Everything is better in Barcelona...".

7.8 Assignments

7.8.1 What You Leave Behind

Imagine you are about to leave your familiar hometown and country, to work or study in a far away country. Name at least 10 things/places/people/activities you will leave behind.

7.8.2 Your Comfort Zone

Some of the above, you will miss very much. Mark them: + Others you will be glad to leave behind. Mark them: – Some of these familiar people and places we take for granted. But in times of distress, which of the above people/things/places would you turn to? Mark them: * They are your social-emotional network.

7.8.3 Creating New Strategies

What are your strategies for building up a new network in the new country?

7.8.4 Your Fellow Students in Culture Shock

Denying culture shock doesn't help. Recognising and managing it is more realistic. Parents, lecturers and fellow students can be a great help in this process. In what way could you help a culture shocked foreign student in your class?

About the Authors

From highly diverse cultural and professional backgrounds, the authors worked together at Utrecht University of Applied Sciences, and decided to write an Intercultural Management book aimed at first and second year university students at international programmes. A book that is accessible, packed with real-life student examples and full of hands-on assignments.

Carlos Nunez is Colombian. He studied Design in Berlin; Architecture at Los Andes University in Bogotá, Colombia; and Urban Planning at Delft University of Technology, in the Netherlands, where he specialised in Decision Making and Computer Modelling. After working in architecture, management and decision making in Colombia, Germany, the Netherlands, and the Ukraine, Carlos developed management simulation games, using cultural diversity as leverage for improved decision making. With his passion for restoring old-timer cars, Carlos created "The Car Race", a simulation game for excellent international team work. He has worked at the Royal Tropical Institute in Amsterdam, training Dutch managers and engineers on international assignments. Carlos lectured at international bachelors and masters programmes at Rotterdam Business School, Utrecht University of Applied Sciences and Bremerhaven University of Applied Sciences. As interim manager, he created an internationalization plan for the School of Technology, at INHOLLAND University in Alkmaar, the Netherlands.

Raya Nunez Mahdi is Indonesian, and grew up in Thailand, China, Indonesia, Russia, the Netherlands and Germany. She studied Cultural Anthropology at the Humboldt University in Berlin, Germany, where she met her husband, Carlos. She completed an English Teachers' Training course in Bogotá Colombia, and studied Social and Medical Anthropology at the University of Amsterdam. After working as an Intercultural Communication trainer at the Royal Tropical Institute in Amsterdam, Raya now lectures Intercultural Management, at Utrecht University of Applied Sciences. She trains lecturers in managing multicultural classrooms more effectively, and is preparing a PhD research on the impact of culture on learning preferences. The results will be used to develop an even more culturally sensitive approach to Competency Based Learning, one that is accessible for students from all cultures. Carlos and Raya Nunez run an Intercultural Management Training Consultancy in The Hague, the Netherlands.

Laura Popma is Dutch and grew up in the Netherlands. She studied Modern English Linguistics at the University of Amsterdam. She then worked as a teacher of English at secondary schools. After various IT courses and a postdoctor-al course in corporate education she worked as an information analyst in the software industry and developed training courses for IT specialists. Laura also trained IT specialists in project management and communication courses. She developed courses in didactics and train-the-trainer courses and trained lecturers in these courses. She now lectures Business Communication Skills, Intercultural Communication and Globalization and Culture at Utrecht University of Applied Sciences.

Bibliography

Adler, N. (2002). *International Dimensions of Organizational Behavior*. Kent: PWS-Kent Publishing Company, 4th edition

Bauer, R. (2006). *Interviews Hogeschool Utrecht -Erasmus Network*. Utrecht: Hogeschool Utrecht

Bennett, J.M. and Bennett, M.J. (2002). *Intercultural Communication for Practitioners*. Winterthur: Zurich UP

Bouaazi, S. (2005). *Intercultureel Management Onderzoek*. Utrecht: Hogeschool Utrecht

Claes, M.T. and Gerritsen, M. (2002). *Culturele Waarden en Communicatie in Internationaal Perspectief*. Bussum: Coutinho

Carabba, M.H. (2002) *Doing Business in Argentina*, Workshop, Royal Tropical Institute, Amsterdam

Hall, E. (1959) *The Silent Language*. Anchor Books Editions, 1990

Hall, E. and Reed Hall, M. (1990). *Understanding Cultural Differences*. Yarmouth: Intercultural Press

Herzberg, F. (1991) *Herzberg on Motivation*, Penton Media Inc

Hofstede, G. (1991). *Cultures and Organizations. Software of the Mind*. New York: McGraw Hill

Hofstede, G. and Hofstede, G.J. and Minkov, M (2010). *Cultures and Organizations, Software of the Mind*. New York: McGraw-Hill Book Company

Hofstede, G. (2010) *"Nog Meer Anders Denkenden"* Announcement of the 6th Dimension Workshop handouts, SIETAR Netherlands, Arnhem, 2 February 2010

Huijser, M. (2006). *The Cultural Advantage. A New Model for Succeeding with Global Teams*. Nicholas Brealey Publishing, London

Inzerilli, G. and Laurent, A. (1979) *The Concept of Organizational Structure*. Working Paper, University of Pennsylvania and INSEAD

Judge, T.A. and Robbins S.P. (2010), *Essentials of Organizational Behavior*, Pearson Education

Kaldenbach, H. (2003). *Doe maar gewoon 99 Tips voor het omgaan met Nederlanders*. Amsterdam: Prometheus

Kaldenbach, H. (2004). *Respect. 99 Tips voor het omgaan met jongeren in de straatcultuur.* Amsterdam: Prometheus

Kiplagat, C. *Interviews Hogeschool Utrecht,* June 2009

KIT, Royal Tropical Institute, Amsterdam (2003). *Module Intercultural Communication*

Kluckhohn, F.R. and Strodtbeck, F.L. (1961). *Variations in Value Orientation.* Evanston: Evanston UP

Kolb, D. (1984). *Experiential Learning. Experience as the Source of Learning and Development.* New Jersey: Prentice Hall Inc

Richard D. Lewis, *When Cultures Collide.* Nicholas Breadley Publishing, London, 3rd edition, 2005

Laurent, A. (1997) *Workshop Blue Cultures, Green Cultures,* SIETAR Poitiers, France

Lewin, K. (1947) Some Social Psychological Differences between the US and Germany. In

McGregor, D. (2006). *The Human Side of Enterprise.* McGraw-Hill Professional

Linden, W.A.M. van der, (2002) Meetings at the IBD. Hogeschool Utrecht

Mooij, M. de. (2005). *Global Marketing and Advertising, Understanding Cultural Paradoxes.* Sage Publications, USA

Minkov, M.(2007) Monumentalism. Workshop for SIETAR Europa, Sofia, Bulgaria

Minkov, M. (2007) *What Makes us Different and Similar.* Klasika I Stil, Sofia, Bulgaria

Mooij, M. de (2005) *Global Marketing and Advertising, Understanding Cultural Paradoxes.* Sage Publications, USA

Nkechi, A. (2009) *Interviews Hogeschool Utrecht.* July 2009

Nunez, C., Nunez, R. and Popma, L. (2006). HOVO Reader: *Interculturele Sensitiviteit.* Utrecht: Hogeschool Utrecht

Nunez. R. (1991). *Dual Careers and International Assignments. First Facts.* Amsterdam

Nunez, R. (2005). *Prescriptum: Cultural Preferences in Learning Styles.* Utrecht

Nunez. R. (1997) *Cultural Perspectives in Sustainable Development,* Working Paper, 5 Jaar na Rio, Locale Agenda 21, Utrecht

Oomkens, F.R. (1994). *Training als beroep. Sociale en Interculturele vaardigheden.* Amsterdam: Boom

Parsons,T and Schils, E.A. (1951) *Towards a General Theory of Action.* Harvard University Press, Cambridge, Mass. USA

Pelto, P.J. (1968) *The Difference between Tight and Loose Societies.* Transaction

Pinto, D. (1994). *Interculturele Communicatie.* Houten: Bohn Stafleu Van Loghum

Pollock, D.C. and Reken, R.E. van (2001) *Third Culture Kids.* Nicholas Brealey Publishing, London

Rotter, J.B. (1966) *Generalised Expectations for Internal versus External Control of Reinforcement.* Psychological Monograph 609

Schein, E.C. (2004). *Organizational Culture and Leadership.* New York: Wiley Publishers, 3rd edition

Shadid, W.A.R. *Beeldvorming. De Verborgen Dimensie bij Interculturele Communicatie.* Tilburg University Press, 1994

Stouffer, S.A. and Toby, J. (1951) *Role Conflict and Personality.* American Journal of Sociology LUI-5, 1951

Tannen, D. (2006). *Je begrijpt me gewoon niet.* Amsterdam: Bert Bakker

Trickey, D and Ewington, N. *A World of Difference, Working Successfully Across Cultures,* DVD and Manual

Trompenaars, F. and Hampden Turner, C. (1998). *Over de Grenzen van Cultuur en Management.* Amsterdam: Business Contact, 3rd edition

Trompenaars, F. and Hampden Turner, C, (2008) *Riding the Waves of Culture. Understanding Cultural Diversity.* 2nd edition. Nicholas Breadly Publishing, London

Trompenaars, F and Woolliams, P. (2011) *Lost in Translation.* Harvard Business Review, April 2011

Vossestein, J. (2004). *Dealing with the Dutch.* KIT Publishers, Amsterdam

Vossestein, J. (1998). Zo werkt dat in Nederland. Amsterdam: KIT Publishers

World Commission Environment and Development, (1987), *Our Common Future,* The Brundtland Report